D0712111

Guide for the Beginning Therapist

Guide for the Beginning Therapist

Relationship Between Diagnosis and Treatment

Amy Lamson, Ph.D.

HUMAN SCIENCES PRESS
72 Fifth Avenue   3 Henrietta Street
NEW YORK, NY 10011 ● LONDON, WC2E 8LU

Library of Congress Catalog Number 78-4061

ISBN: 0-87705-367-7

Printed in the United States of America
89 987654321

Library of Congress Cataloging in Publication Data

Lamson, Amy
    Guide for the beginning therapist.

    Bibliography
    Includes index.
    1. Psychotherapy. 2. Diagnosis, Differential. 3. Mental illness-Diagnosis.
I. Title. [DNLM: 1. Mental disorders-Diagnosis. 2. Psychotherapy. WM420.3
L241g]
RC480.5.L34   616.8'9   78-4061
ISBN 0-87705-367-7

Dedicated to my family

CONTENTS

7

PREFACE

It has been many decades since the practice of psychotherapy was confined to the psychiatric profession. Society's increasing demand for psychotherapy beyond the capacity of the limited supply of psychiatrists has forced psychiatrists to share their therapeutic role with other mental health professionals. Psychologists' skill in diagnosing mental disorders won them the opportunity of treating these same disorders. Social workers' effectiveness in counseling relatives of patients won them the opportunity of treating the patient's themselves. For many years these three groups of professionals were the mainstay of the mental health field. Then, when the demand for psychotherapy exceeded even this supply, it became necessary to extend the practice of psychotherapy to other helping professionals, such as nurses, educators, and pastors, with some training in mental health concepts. It was not long before these fields developed special training programs in psychotherapy.

It soon became obvious that successful treatment depends more on the nature of the therapeutic relationship than on the therapist's particular professional background. With this realization and with the pressures of large numbers of untreated psychiatric inpatients, mental hospitals started permitting hospital personnel with a lot of practical experience in dealing with these patients, but without formal training in therapy, to meet with patients in individual therapy sessions. The philosophy behind this practice was that an individual therapeutic relationship with an untrained therapist is better than none at all. In many cases the good will and common sense of the untrained therapist supported this claim. More recently, community and rehabilitation treatment centers started hiring community members and successfully rehabilitated persons to serve as paraprofessional therapists. It was felt that paraprofessionals coming from backgrounds similar to those of their clients would be especially qualified to understand and relate to their clients. In many cases this proved to be true.

The discovery of the effectiveness of therapists without formal training naturally had an effect on the whole field of mental health. Professionals and nonprofessionals alike began to question the value of formal training. As a result, in recent years there has been a movement away from rigorous training in basic clinical knowledge. In my view this is unfortunate. Although the therapeutic relationship is the major factor in successful treatment, clinical understanding is also essential. Although some gifted persons have enough intuitive insight to become good therapists without formal training, most beginning therapists cannot. Moreover, even those gifted persons can increase their therapeutic skill by increasing their clinical knowledge.

With all this in mind, it appears to me that it is time to reverse the recent trend away from basic clinical training. This book has been written in an easy-to-digest style and format for the rapidly expanding population of beginning therapists from all backgrounds who need more exposure to basic clinical concepts in diagnosis and treatment.

ACKNOWLEDGMENTS

First, I would like to express my gratitude to all my teachers, supervisors, and colleagues who have contributed to my clinical understanding. I also want to express my deep appreciation of the patients described in this book for their courage and hard work in therapy.

In addition, I want to thank all the trainees who attended my Psychopathology Seminars at Trinity Mental Health Center in Framingham, Massachusetts, from 1972 to 1974, and at the Charles Drew Family Life Center in Dorchester, Massachusetts, from 1974 to 1975, for their enthusiastic response to the seminars which inspired the writing of this book.

My gratitude also goes to my colleague and friend, Sandra Ceren, Ph.D., for her encouragement and helpful suggestions in the writing of this book, and to my neighbor and friend, author Peggy Durdin, for graciously offering to edit my writing and for her encouragement and suggestions regarding publication.

Finally, I want to thank Joy Simpson for her patience and care in typing the manuscript.

INTRODUCTION

As the title indicates, this book has been written with the beginning therapist in mind. Unlike many books written for experienced therapists which propose new theories and treatment methods or discuss particular syndromes in depth, this book is aimed at presenting basic clinical knowledge about the diagnosis and treatment of a wide range of clinical problems. As such, it draws upon many different theories of psychotherapy and attempts to indicate the best application of these theories. This book also draws upon my own clinical experience and certain practical techniques of treatment that I have found to be very useful

In my view every school of therapy has something to offer, but no school of therapy has all the answers. Therefore the therapeutic approach for each case should be dictated more by the nature of the patient's problems than by a particular theoretical orientation. In other words, treatment should be tailored to meet the needs of the patient by selecting and combining the most suitable methods from a variety of sources. Obviously this approach to treatment requires a careful diagnosis of the patient's problem.

The purpose of this book is to demonstrate through discussion and case presentations the importance of diagnosis in treatment and how various methods from different schools of therapy can be combined for the effective treatment of different clinical syndromes.

Effective treatment refers here to improvement in the patient's functioning and self-esteem, rather than to a total cure of the patient's problems. It is my belief that no one can be totally cured for the simple reason that no one can be totally free of problems. All that we can strive for in therapy is to diminish the patient's problems and to improve the patient's ability to cope with those that do remain or will appear in the future.

In keeping with the practical aims of this book, every attempt has been made to use simple, everyday language and to avoid psychological jargon. There will be very little footnoting because the ideas culled from my various readings have become so much a part of me that it is frequently impossible for me to isolate the source of each idea. The bibliography at the back of the book is a compilation of the readings that have had the greatest influence on my clinical thinking. The readings preceded by asterisks are the ones I recommend most highly for the beginning therapist.

One more point has to be made at the start of this book. After experimenting with several different ways of avoiding the exclusive use of masculine pronouns to stand for both male and female, I have decided that the simplest solution is to alternate masculine and feminine pronouns chapter by chapter. In each case it should be understood that the pronoun stands for both male and female.

Chapter 1

DIAGNOSIS

IMPORTANCE OF DIAGNOSIS

Psychiatric diagnostic classifications help the therapist to assess the seriousness of the patient's problems and to determine how to proceed in therapy. A failure to diagnose properly the essential problem can considerably slow down treatment, if not impede it altogether.

For example, in treating a juvenile delinquent it is crucial to determine whether the antisocial behavior is primarily motivated by hostile impulses or an excessive need for approval by the peer group. In treating depression, it is important to determine whether the patient's low self-esteem arises primarily out of guilt feelings or a sense of inadequacy. In treating a patient who permits others to abuse her, it is necessary to determine whether the patient welcomes the abuse or simply doesn't know how to avoid it. In treating a sexual problem, it is necessary to determine whether it is the result of deep-seated inhibition, or a lack of information and experience, or a problem in the relationship.

It is obvious from these examples that effective treatment does depend on a thorough understanding of the problem. A description of the behavior is not enough because the same behavior can represent many different underlying problems. In each case it is essential to determine the underlying problem as well as the underlying strengths.

Thus far we have considered the possibility of ineffective treatment. Far more serious is the possibility of maltreatment due to lack of proper diagnosis and treatment plan. For example, if a preschizophrenic's vulnerability is not recognized and she is treated like a neurotic, the treatment itself can precipitate a psychosis. On the other hand, if a normal childhood developmental problem is mistakenly interpreted as a serious emotional disorder, the unnecessary stress placed on the parents could very well exacerbate the child's problem. If the confusion and disorganization of a patient with an undetected brain tumor is treated psychologically, the treatment is a wasted effort and valuable time is lost. If a patient's suicidal or homicidal tendencies are not fully recognized, it is likely that she will be released from treatment too soon and will eventually harm someone. It is abundantly clear from these examples that it is absolutely necessary to diagnose correctly a patient's problem to provide the appropriate treatment.

In recent years the use of psychiatric diagnostic classifications has been under severe attack. According to its critics, psychiatric diagnosis is at best a waste of time when trying to help people with their problems, and at worst, a real menace to the people supposedly being helped. The critics believe psychiatric diagnoses are artificial abstractions that say little about an individual's problems and as such are useless in the attempt to understand people. The critics of psychiatric diagnoses also point out how they can hinder treatment when they are used as a substitute for true understanding. Finally, these critics assert that the prognoses and underlying moral judgments associated with many diagnoses actually harm many patients.

While recognizing some merit in these criticisms of the use of psychiatric diagnoses, the author strongly believes the critics are going too far in wishing to discard them altogether. They have failed to distinguish between the intrinsic merit in psychiatric diagnoses and their misuse.

First of all, the critics have failed to recognize that diagnosis is more than simple classification. The classification is the end result of the whole diagnostic process, which includes the patient's history, dynamics, strengths, and weaknesses. It pulls together all the data about the patient into a meaningful abstraction that has important implications for treatment. But it is by no means a substitute for a full understanding of the patient.

As for the criticism regarding prognoses, it should be remembered that no prognosis, as indeed no diagnosis, is absolute. Both can change with time. In fact, with effective therapy, they often do. Therefore every patient should be accorded the best possible treatment and the therapist should look upon a negative prognosis as an extra challenge.

Finally, it is unfortunate that moral judgments have been associated with certain diagnoses. However, moral judgments are not a necessary condition of the traditional psychiatric diagnosis. The issue is not the diagnoses themselves, but the attitudes of those using them. The therapist should recognize that a patient's deviant behavior is her indirect and frequently unsuccessful attempt to fulfill basic human needs that, for some reason, have not been fulfilled in more usual ways. As long as the therapist keeps this in mind and recognizes her common humanity with the patient, she will concentrate on helping the patient learn how to achieve greater satisfaction in life and not on rendering harsh judgments about deviant behavior.

How to Make a Diagnosis

Before one can begin to make psychiatric diagnoses, one must be thoroughly familiar with the various diagnostic categories. To achieve this one must carefully study written descriptions of the different diagnoses and accompanying case histories in various textbooks. Then it is a good idea to review one's knowledge by studying the *Diagnostic and Statistical Manual of Mental Disorders*, published by the American Psychiatric Association. In addition, one should attend diagnostic conferences to observe the process of diagnosis and the uniting of academic knowledge with actual experience.

Once one has a solid understanding of the different psychiatric classifications, one can interview a patient for the purpose of establishing a diagnosis. While asking questions and recording the patient's answers about the presenting complaint, the background of the problem, and the patient's history, the therapist must closely observe the patient and ask herself the following questions:

Is the patient's mood elevated or depressed? If so, to what degree?

Does the patient's affect tend to be flat or labile?

Does the patient display extreme anxiety?

Are the patient's conflicts internalized or externalized?

How organized is her thinking?

Has she displayed good or poor judgment in her past behavior?

Does she show good or poor insight into her present difficulties?

Are there any signs of confusion, irrational thinking, delusions, or hallucinations?

The answers to these questions can tell a lot about the patient. Here are some examples:

A person who is generally well liked and respected by others, but is troubled by severe emotional conflicts, is undoubtedly neurotic. On the other hand, a person who repeatedly comes into conflict with others, but has little sense of inner conflict, probably has .a personality or character disorder.

An emotionally labile, impulsive, trusting individual is likely to have an hysterical neurosis or neurotic character, in contrast to an emotionally reserved, overcautious, indecisive individual who is likely to have an obsessive neurosis or neurotic character.

A severely depressed individual who is confused and reproaches herself irrationally is likely to be psychotically depressed, whereas the depressed person who is overwhelmed by a loss, but not irrational, is likely to be neurotically depressed.

Illogical thinking combined with severe anxiety very likely signifies an incipient schizophrenic condition, whereas the same illogical thinking with flat affect signifies fully developed schizophrenia.

A patient who distorts reality, but reaches out for a relationship is more likely to be a borderline psychotic rather than schizophrenic.

Of course, the diagnosis is not always immediately obvious from observation alone. That is why it is necessary to take a

careful history of the patient's presenting complaint to determine (1) time of onset, (2) precipitating events or stresses,
(3) mode of onset (gradual or sudden), and (4) extent of
incapacity related to the symptoms.

Here are two examples of how the answers to these questions can differentiate a diagnosis:

> Depression following a loss is likely to be neurotic, where-
> as depression that is cyclic is likely to be part of the person-
> ality (cyclothymic personality) or, depending upon the
> severity, even psychotic.

> A gradual break with reality in the early teens without any
> specific precipitating event is probably a simple schizo-
> phrenia that will very likely be chronic. A sudden break
> with reality in the late teens following a precipitating event
> is most likely acute schizophrenic reaction with a good
> chance of recovery.

Up to this point we have considered only differential
diagnoses between similar, yet mutually exclusive syndromes. But suppose a patient displays symptoms from
two different, yet compatible syndromes, for example,
neurotic depression and passive-dependent behavior. In
this case one can include both syndromes in the diagnosis,
placing the most dominant feature first, for example,
"passive-dependent personality with depressive trends"
or "depressive neurosis in a passive-dependent personality."

DIAGNOSTIC CATEGORIES

Before proceeding to specific diagnoses and the treatment of
specific cases, let us consider the major diagnostic categories
and the major focus of treatment for each.

Neurosis

A neurotic is an individual whose overall functioning is fairly
good, but who has difficulties which may be temporary or in

specific areas of functioning. Neurosis arises out of intra-psychic (inner) tension and conflict and is manifested in three major ways: reactive neurosis, symptom neurosis, and character neurosis.

A neurosis can be a temporary emotional reaction to stress, as in the anxiety reactions and reactive depressions that occur in all personality types and are probably the most common presenting complaints.

A neurosis can be a symptom representing a compromise between impulse and defense which is associated with enduring personality traits, as in the conversion reaction of an hysterical personality and the compulsive hand washing of an obsessive-compulsive personality.

Finally, a neurosis can pervade the personality and behavior of the individual to such a degree that it exists even when there is no particular stress and no specific symptoms, as in (1) the hysterical neurotic character who strongly represses any cognitive awareness of inner conflict, (2) the obsessive-compulsive neurotic character who responds to inner conflict with intellectualization and isolation of affect, and (3) the depressive neurotic character who interprets every experience in the most negative, pessimistic way possible.

The reactive and symptom neuroses are *ego-alien* because they are regarded by the individual as unwelcome intrusions. A character neurosis is *ego-syntonic* because it is so much a part of the individual that she feels quite at home with it. All three kinds of neurosis are *autoplastic* because they bring about changes in the individual.

A question may arise over the difference between an hysterical (or obsessive-compulsive) *personality*, on the one hand, and an hysterical (or obsessive-compulsive) *character*, on the other. Although many clinicians make no distinction between them, it is the author's opinion that the former terms should be reserved for basically healthy individuals whose personality traits do not *usually* interfere with their functioning. The character neurosis designation, on the other hand, should be used for individuals with neurotic personality traits that do impair their functioning in certain ways.

Of the three types of neuroses, reactive neuroses are easiest to treat because they are of recent onset and have not solidified into a permanent part of the personality structure. Secondly, they have specific precipitants which makes them rather readily understood. Thirdly, they are temporary, and thus bound to improve, even without treatment, though of course treatment should speed up recovery. Therefore it is not surprising that reactive neuroses are successfully treated by a variety of approaches. In many cases supportive therapies are sufficient for immediate relief of the neurotic reaction. Insight therapies take longer, but they have the advantage of making the individual better able to cope with future stress.

Character neuroses are the most difficult neuroses to treat because of their long-standing, pervasive nature, which makes it difficult for the individual to pinpoint the problem. Character neuroses usually require long-term insight therapy to uncover the unconscious basis of neurotic behavior.

Symptom neurosis stand between reactive and character neuroses in the length of treatment and the necessity of insight for change. Although insight therapy has traditionally been the treatment of choice in symptom neuroses, there are cases where insight is neither necessary nor sufficient to produce change, and in such cases behavior therapy is more effective. This is particularly true for phobias, which respond very well to systematic desensitization, and also for obsessive thinking, which responds very well to thought stopping.

Psychosomatic Reactions

A psychosomatic reaction is a physical expression of enduring emotional tension. This is in contrast to an hysterical conversion reaction, which is a symbolic expression of a specific emotional conflict, and with a hypochondriacal reaction, which involves fear of illness, preoccupation with bodily functions, and exaggerated attention to physical discomforts.

According to psychoanalytic theory, each psychosomatic reaction has a specific dynamic etiology. For example, asthma represents a suppressed cry for the mother, ulcers represent unfulfilled dependency needs, and high blood pressure represents suppressed anger. According to the constitutional theory, psychosomatic reactions reflect general emotional tension and a genetic factor determines which organ is affected. Current psychiatric thinking regards both genetic and dynamic factors as involved in psychosomatic reactions. In some cases genetic factors predominate, while in other cases, dynamic factors predominate.

The person with a psychosomatic reaction typically has great difficulty handling feelings and tends to defend against them by denial, repression and isolation. If a person's emotions are continuously blocked by rigid psychological defenses, they eventually find release through bodily symptoms. These people need to learn how to deal with the emotions more effectively, but their rigid defenses against recognizing emotions makes them extremely resistant to therapy. They almost never seek therapy on their own and when they are referred, they come reluctantly, if at all. Once in therapy they focus on their physical complaints and often terminate after a few sessions because they can't think of anything more to say and there has been no improvement in their physical symptoms. In order for therapy to take place, the therapist must skillfully engage the patient in treatment, first by establishing therapeutic rapport, and then by persistent redirection of the patient's attention away from his physical symptoms toward significant relationships in his life. By this means the patient will gradually recognize his emotional difficulties and, with the support and guidance of the therapist, will learn how to deal with them more effectively.

Personality and Character Disorders

The terms *personality disorder* and *character disorder* are used interchangeably to designate a wide range of behavior disorders (the term used in work with children) that bring the individual into conflict with others. The individual experiences little, if any, inner conflict and basically sees nothing wrong with her behavior. Therefore this is an *ego-syntonic* disorder. It is also an *alloplastic* disorder because the individual tries to manipulate the behavior of others to suit her own needs. Only when conflict with others jeopardizes the fulfillment of her needs, does the individual become emotionally upset. In other words, as long as there are no external obstacles to her wishes, the individual appears quite happy. This is in contrast to the neurotic who suffers inwardly even in the absence of external difficulties. On the other hand, the neurotic generally has a higher level of general functioning than a person with a personality or character disorder.

It should be noted that although these distinctions are helpful in evaluating a patient's major difficulties, they are not absolute. People with personality and character disorders can experience neurotic anxiety and depression at times. What is significant is that for them this is a relatively infrequent, short-lived, and superficial experience. Similarly, neurotics can and do experience conflicts with others, but they are not nearly as deep or involved as the conflicts they have with themselves.

Although the terms *personality disorder* and *character disorder* are used interchangeably, in the author's opinion the former should be reserved for personality weaknesses such as passive-dependency, passive-aggressiveness, immaturity, and inadequacy, whereas the latter should be reserved for impulse disorders such as impulsive and unstable behavior, alcoholism, drug addiction, sexual perversions, uncontrolled explosive anger, and antisocial attitudes and behavior. Narcissism shows features of both categories.

Persons with personality disorders are generally more interested in treatment because they find little satisfaction in life, whereas persons with character disorders do find satisfaction in their deviant way. However, it should be noted that as much as they avoid inner conflict, persons with character disorders are not without suffering. If they are confronted with the ways in which their behavior causes them pain, they will be more amenable to treatment. Thus, to some degree, treatment is aimed at increasing the anxiety of patients with character disorders, in contrast to the treatment of neurotics, which is aimed at decreasing anxiety.

Both personality and character disorder patients require a great deal of guidance and support to improve their level of functioning, with insight playing a secondary role. In general, treatment of the personality disorders should be aimed at increasing their ego strength and self-confidence so that they can function on a more independent, mature level. In the case of the narcissistic personality disorder, the incongruency between the individual's grandiose expectations and the sense of entitlement on the one hand, and her unrealistically low self-esteem on the other, should be indicated repeatedly so that she can arrive at a more realistic, moderate view of herself. Treatment of the character disorders should be focussed on the negative consequences of her behavior. Once the patient's concern is aroused, she will be ready to learn how to control behavior that is harmful to herself. In the process she will also be controlling behavior harmful to others.

Borderline Personality

Borderline personalities border on all the other diagnostic

categories and as such display all kinds of pathology. However the essence of the borderline syndrome is a nearly psychotic ego defect, with primitive fantasies entering consciousness, but no formal thought disorder. Brief transitory psychotic episodes may occur, but reality always reasserts itself and the borderline personality never develops a full-fledged psychosis. Borderline personalities may be classified by their predominant feature, such as schizoid, paranoid, cyclothymic, oral-hysteric, or they may be referred to simply as borderline. Treatment of these patients should be directed toward practical reality and the strengthening of ego controls over thought and behavior. In many ways the treatment of the borderline is the opposite of the treatment of the neurotic, where the aim is uncovering unconscious fantasies underlying behavior. Here the aim is to cover up and suppress the nearly psychotic fantasies, not to develop insight about them.

Psychoses

Psychosis involves a break with reality that can occur in thoughts or feelings. Schizophrenia is the psychotic *thought* disorder, and manic-depression and psychotic depression are psychotic *affect* disorders. Postpartum (after childbirth) and involutional (midlife) psychoses can be of either type and it is debatable whether they should be considered separate entities. Although it is important to note their unique circumstances, in the author's opinion they are not fundamentally different from the major thought and affect psychoses.

In a thought disorder, thinking has lost its normal reference to reality and is out of control. Some or all of the following symptoms may develop: distorted perceptions, irrational ideas, bizarre fantasies, illogical reasoning, and peculiar language. Medication is very effective in suppressing schizophrenic thinking, but it is not ideal as a permanent treatment because of the many undesirable side effects. Psychotherapy is needed to help the patient learn to cope with her problems. Patients in the early states of schizophrenia are frightened by the invasion of primary process thinking into consciousness and will accept a therapist's clarification of reality and suggestions for testing reality. But in the later stages, schizophrenics blandly accept their primary

   process thinking (because it has become ego-syntonic) and they will strongly resist any direct attempt to bring them back to reality.

   In working with these patients it is necessary to use indirect means of bringing them back to reality by establishing a friendly, supportive relationship and by engaging them in discussions of practical, everyday issues while avoiding discussions of their irrational notions. In this way the patient will gain more interest and satisfaction in reality and gradually lose her involvement in schizophrenic thinking.

   In an affect disorder, feelings have lost their normal reference to reality and are out of control. The patient's interpretation of events is distorted so that she will respond with intense joy or sadness to things that normally produce a milder reaction. In addition, judgment of appropriate behavior is very poor, so that she will behave, without any apparent concern, in ways that would normally produce great embarrassment. Despite these aberrations in affect and behavior, the patient displays none of the extremely illogical, peculiar features of a formal thought disorder. Medication is very helpful to suppress the extreme emotional reactions, but psychotherapy is also needed to help the patient come to terms with whatever disappointments underly them.

Chapter 2

THERAPY

WHAT IS PSYCHOTHERAPY?

There are many forms of psychotherapy and there are many therapeutic encounters that occur outside of psychotherapy. Therefore there is no simple definition of psychotherapy. One way to arrive at an understanding of the essential nature of psychotherapy is to consider various aspects of it and then to compare it to the similar, yet different experience of friendship.

1. Psychotherapy is an interaction between T (therapist) and P (patient).

2. Its purpose is for T to help P cope with problems and find greater satisfaction in life.

3. T is not involved in P's problems and therefore can have a more objective perspective on P's problems than P or anyone closely involved with P.

4. T has special training and experience to understand and help people with their problems.

5. T tries to help P with problems in the following ways:

   a) by increasing P's insight into his problems through questions, clarifications, reflection, and interpretation;

   b) by offering guidance through information and by suggesting alternatives;

   c) by supporting P emotionally through reassurance and encouragement.

Friendship is also an interaction between two people, but unlike therapy it is not designed for the benefit of one party. Friendship is a mutual give-and-take relationship. A friend might be a good sounding board for one's feelings and might give a new perspective on a problem, but a friend cannot be as objective as a trained therapist with whom one is not personally involved. In most instances a friend's interest and advice are sufficient help for a problem. But in some cases the problem is too complex or too deep-seated to be adequately handled in this manner. That is when the special skills of a trained therapist are needed.

CHARACTERISTICS OF AN EFFECTIVE THERAPIST

In trying to comprehend how psychotherapy actually works, the author has tried to evaluate how much the therapist's personality, training, and experience contribute to the success of treatment. It is the author's opinion that successful treatment depends upon all three attributes. A genuinely caring and empathic personality is necessary for the establishment of a therapeutic relationship, which is the basis of any therapeutic work. Training is necessary to provide a cognitive framework for understanding patients' problems. Finally, experience is necessary to develop both the practical know-how in handling these problems and the confidence that one has the know-how.

THE THERAPEUTIC RELATIONSHIP

The first step in treating any patient is the establishment of a therapeutic relationship. Precisely what constitutes a therapeutic relationship varies from patient to patient and from therapist to therapist. That is why some therapists can work only with certain types of patients and vice versa. In some cases the therapeutic relationship may be warm and friendly. In other cases it may be very respectful. In general it can be stated that for a neurotic patient, the most impor-that factor is faith in the therapist's competence; for the patient with a personality or character disorder, it is the be-lief that the therapist basically likes him; and for the psy-chotic, it is trust in the therapist's dependability. But in all cases the patient must feel accepted by the therapist before any therapeutic work can begin.

Depending upon the patient, the therapist can demon-strate acceptance in any number of ways. If the patient is anxious for sympathy and understanding, the therapist can demonstrate acceptance by sympathetically listening to the patient's problems before confronting the patient with ways he has contributed to his problems. If the patient is anxious to avoid discussing his problem, the therapist can demon-strate acceptance by discovering the patient's interests before bringing the discussion to the patient's problems. In each case the therapist should be attuned to what the patient needs to become comfortable in the therapeutic setting and to become open to treatment.

SCHOOLS OF THERAPY

There are many different schools of therapy in practice today, each reporting great success with its particular methods of treatment. Over the years the author has made the following observations:

1. Each school of therapy has something of value to offer in the treatment of emotional problems.

2. No school is the answer to all problems.

3. Each school is best suited to treat certain types of problems.

4. In practice, the different schools are not as different as their supporters claim. They have many things in common that they often overlook. Their main differences are what they choose to emphasize.

The author has also reached the conclusion that treatment should be tailored to the specific problem by selecting and combining suitable methods from the various schools of therapy. In fact it is the purpose of this book to demonstrate this selective approach to the treatment of the various diagnostic categories.

Since beginning therapists should already be well acquainted with the various schools of therapy, all that will be presented here is a table of the main features of the five schools that have had the greatest influence on the author's therapeutic thinking and practice.

School	Founder and Background	Cause of Symptoms	Treatment Goals	Treatment Method
Psycho-analytic	Freud (neuro-psychiatry)	Unconscious conflicts from the past	Uncover unconscious conflicts	Free association and interpretations of dreams and past experiences
Transactional analysis	Berne (psychoanalytic)	Acceptance of self-defeating social roles and life scripts	Alter social roles and life scripts	Analyze current interactions with others
Gestalt	Perls (psycho-analytic)	True feelings are blocked from aware-ness	Get in touch with feelings	Act out feelings; focus on immediate reactions to situations
Rational-emotive	Ellis (psycho-analytic)	Irrational thinking	Change way of thinking	Reasoning, homework assignments
Behavior	Wolpe (experimental psychology)	Conditioned habits	Remove symptoms	Decon-ditioning

Chapter 3

ANXIETY

CLINICAL DESCRIPTION

Anxiety is an inborn, involuntary physiological reaction to danger that appears at the time of birth and reappears throughout life whenever the individual perceives a threat to her well being, such as possible loss of financial security, possible loss of love, and possible loss of self-esteem. The anxiety reaction, including rapid heart beat, sudden changes in blood flow, and drying of mucous membranes, is mediated by the sympathetic division of the autonomic nervous system. Associated with these physiological reactions are feelings of dread, apprehension, and fear. Although anxiety is usually viewed as very undesirable, it should be remembered that anxiety is a valuable warning system. It mobilizes the individual to deal with danger. It is undesirable only when it becomes so extreme that it paralyzes the individual into a state of helplessness. Freud called the former *normal anxiety* and the latter *neurotic anxiety,* which he considered the basis of all neurosis.

It is important to keep this distinction in mind when treating patients for anxiety. The goal of treatment should not be the elimination of all anxiety. A certain amount of normal anxiety is necessary for adequate functioning, and toleration of it is a sign of maturity. People without any, or hardly any, anxiety have character disorders. They lack normal concern about the consequences of their behavior, and as a result they act in ways that harm themselves and others. In working with neurotics the goal of a treatment should be the elimination of neurotic anxiety and increased toleration of normal anxiety.

If neurotic anxiety persists, it may lead to neurotic symptoms which are compromises between unacceptable impulses and the defenses against these impulses. In other cases continued anxiety leads to psychosomatic symptoms. Psychoneurotic and psychosomatic symptoms are attempts to bind the anxiety. Unfortunately one symptom is often not enough to bind the anxiety, and as a result more and more symptoms develop.

Simply being able to talk to someone who is interested and concerned can lessen anxiety somewhat, and indeed this is the beginning of any successful treatment. Here is a description of three widely used methods of treating anxiety, together with their advantages and disadvantages.

ANALYTIC TREATMENT OF ANXIETY

In psychoanalytic therapy, the patient free associates to situations which arouse anxiety so as to uncover its unconscious sources. Once these are fully understood, the anxiety should disappear. The advantage of this method is that it leads to a better understanding of the self and to a greater capacity to cope with future stress. The disadvantage is that it takes a long time and it doesn't work in every case. Some patients are either unwilling or unable to delve deep enough into their unconscious to discover the sources of their neurotic anxiety, and even when these sources are discovered, the insight doesn't always automatically end the anxiety.

RATIONAL-EMOTIVE TREATMENT OF ANXIETY

In rational-emotive therapy, the therapist uncovers the irrational thinking that underlies the patients' anxiety and points out how the patient "catastrophizes" minor problems into major ones. After separating the patient's irrational fears from reasonable concerns, the therapist gives homework assignments to help the patient learn how to deal constructively with her problems. The advantage of this method is that it is fairly quick, yet gives the patient some understanding of her mental processes which she can apply to future situations. The drawback is that merely identifying the irrational thinking doesn't necessarily allay anxiety.

BEHAVIOR TREATMENT OF ANXIETY

Behavior therapy eliminates anxiety by a process of deconditioning. The first step is to teach the patient how to relax physically by successively tightening and relaxing all the muscles of the body and breathing deeply. Later on, whenever the patient feels herself becoming tense, she repeats the relaxation exercise. After a while the exercise can be shortened to deep breathing. If the patient has a specific phobia, this exercise can be practiced as the patient gradually approaches the feared object. This step-by-step desensitization can be accomplished first in fantasy by establishing a mental hierarchy of fears associated with the phobia; then it can be done in vivo, i.e., in real life. Thought stopping is another behavior technique that is very effective in combating anxiety due to obsessive thinking. The patient is taught to say "stop" to herself whenever the obsessive thought pops into mind. At first she might be saying "stop" very frequently, but in a short while it will be necessary only occasionally because the word "stop" interferes with the obsessive thought and breaks the repetitive cycle. In many cases behavior therapy is the most rapid and effective treatment of anxiety. Moreover, though it does not lead to real understanding, the patient can learn to apply the methods to new situations. The disadvantage of this method is that is some cases new symptoms may develop in place of the old symptoms because the underlying problem has not been resolved.

Therapists should select the method or methods of treatment most suitable for each case. The following case example shows how several therapeutic approaches were combined to rid a patient of long-standing, paralyzing anxiety.

CASE REPORT OF AN ANXIETY-RIDDEN PATIENT

The patient was a 28-year-old married man and father of two who wanted treatment for recurring anxiety attacks that had started 6 years before, when he was in the army. He had no idea what brought on these attacks, and it bothered him greatly that he had no control over them. The patient avoided socializing because he worried about having an anxiety attack in the midst of a group. He enjoyed his work in a relative's business, but was frustrated by the low and sometimes delayed pay. The precipitant to his seeking therapy was the news that his son was terminally ill. The patient was extremely attached to this child, who was named after him, and he feared that he might fall apart once the boy died.

During the next two and a half years, while the patient was being seen in therapy, his son's illness and death were never far from the center of his thoughts. Accordingly, much therapy time was devoted to his coming to terms with these painful events. That these discussions were helpful was demonstrated by his reaction at the time of his son's death: he was able to experience his grief fully without being overwhelmed by it.

Throughout treatment there was also a great deal of discussion about the circumstances of his anxiety attacks. Although they could happen at any time, even when he was not particularly tense, it became clear that they were usually associated with a conflict about asserting himself. The patient would feel it necessary to assert himself to protect his rights and his dignity, but he also feared the possible negative consequences of such actions. His anxiety attacks would usually remove him from the possibility of asserting himself, with the result that his anxiety would rapidly diminish and he would be free of any symptoms until the next situation arose in which he felt the need to be assertive. Whenever possible, the patient would avoid situations that would call forth his need to be assertive, and he became more passive than ever. The patient hated his passivity and wished that he could be free of his fears and become more active. But his anxiety attacks terrified him. During them he felt that he was dying or going crazy and he wanted to avoid them at all costs.

When the patient gained some understanding of the cause and function of his anxiety attacks, they were reduced in frequency, but not totally eliminated. At this point the therapist had to decide whether to probe for deeper insight into the origin of his conflicts (perhaps to uncover unconscious castration fears) or to use reasoning and behavior techniques to rid him of these episodes. In view of the emotional strain he was undergoing in connection with his son's death, the therapist decided to take the latter, more supportive approach.

Accordingly, the therapist reasoned with the patient about how unlikely it was that he would die or go crazy during one of his attacks. For one thing, many people have the same feeling during anxiety attacks without dying or going crazy. For another, if the patient were going to die or go crazy from an attack, he had had ample opportunity and it would have happened already. Therefore there was no legitimate reason for him to be so terrified by these episodes. Moreover, his fears about them made them even worse. The patient accepted this line of reasoning and he gave up his hypochondriacal fears about these attacks. Subsequently, his attacks were reduced in severity, but again they did not disappear altogether.

The patient was also encouraged to assert himself more to increase his self-respect, as well as to learn that appropriate self-assertion does not lead to disaster. On the contrary, he would probably be much better off if he stood up for his rights. After years of quietly accepting his low and uncertain pay, which he felt was the result of his relative's poor management, he got up enough courage to speak to his relative about leasing a part of the business to manage on his own. To his great surprise and relief, his relative readily agreed to his terms and indicated that as he got older he would be willing to sell more and more of the business to the patient. In less than a year the patient had completely paid off the sizable loan he needed to get his business started and, though the business was in its seasonal slump, he was earning considerably more than he had earned before. The patient naturally felt very good about this. However he was still not completely free from his anxiety attacks.

By this time the attacks occurred almost exclusively when he was faced with the necessity of interacting with a group of people in social or business situations. He managed to prevent these episodes as much as possible by simply avoiding these situations. There were, however, times when this was impossible; then he would take a tranquilizer which would reduce his anxiety, but not completely eliminate it. The patient wasn't happy with this solution because he wasn't proud of himself for avoiding groups and for being dependent on medication. The therapist expressed the view that at this point the main problem was not the anxiety attacks, but his fear of them and his avoidance of anxiety-producing situations which only reinforced his fear. The patient agreed with this view and accepted the therapist's advice that he force himself to go through with these situations without medication, all the time taking deep breaths and telling himself that it wouldn't be the end of world if he had an anxiety attack and that he would recover without any real harm to himself.

When the patient first followed this advice he found that he was still having his attacks, but they were not as bad as he feared. Furthermore, he quickly recovered from them. In a short while his anxiety reactions were so mild, they couldn't even be called attacks. Even though he was very pleased with his progress, he asked when he would be completely free of anxiety. The therapist told him that repeated mastery of these formerly upsetting situations would further diminish his anxiety, but he could never be totally free of anxiety because some anxiety is normal. Though he wasn't too pleased with this idea, the patient accepted it and the therapy sessions were phased out over the next few months without any need to resume intensive treatment.

Chapter 4

DEPRESSION

CLINICAL DESCRIPTION

Mourning is the normal reaction to any important loss, whether it is an external object or an internal object. This reaction consists of a mingling of sadness over the loss and anger at the loss. In addition, there may be a feeling of inner emptiness or a feeling that the world is an empty place. Several physiological reactions, including loss of appetite, insomnia, and psychomotor retardation (slowing down) may accompany these psychological reactions to loss. Normally these reactions gradually diminish in time as new objects and new ideals take the place of the lost objects and ideals. In some cases, however, these reactions persist long after the loss. When this happens the reaction can be termed a clinical depression. Upon close examination it can be seen that depression involves a severe lowering of self-esteem along with the real loss. That is why recovery is not a simple matter of replacing the lost object or ideal.

FREUDIAN AND EGO-PSYCHOLOGY INTERPRETATIONS OF DEPRESSION

In Freudian psychoanalysis the lowering of self-esteem is interpreted as anger turned inward, i.e., anger at the loss is redirected toward the self. The newer psychoanalytic ego-psychology view is that the lowering of self-esteem in depression is a feeling of helplessness and hopelessness in the face of loss that does not always involve anger turned inward. In any event, the loss of self-esteem can range from guilt and self-blame for the loss to feelings of utter worthlessness. In this regard it is interesting to note how the depressed patient contrasts with the paranoid patient. Whereas the former introjects blame for his problems and feels sad about them, the latter projects blame for his problems onto other people and feels mad about them. In treating the depressed patient it is often important to point out the underlying anger. On the other hand, in treating the paranoid patient, it is often important to point out the underlying sadness.

DEFENSES AGAINST DEPRESSION

Paranoid reactions are not the only defense against depression. Overindulgence of impulses, as in overeating, alcoholism, drug addiction, sexual promiscuity, buying sprees, and kleptomania, can also be defenses against depression. In all these cases the individual "feeds" himself to make up symbolically for the loss he has experienced. Although these behaviors do make the individual feel better for a time, unfortunately they may lead to other problems. In treating these impulse behavior disorders, it is necessary to help the individual get in touch with his underlying depression and learn how to bear it and cope with it in more constructive ways.

Manic behavior is another defense against depression. In a manic reaction the individual defensively denies his sadness defensive reversal and then goes to the other extreme of gladness to convince himself that he is not actually sad (reaction formation). The manic reaction can be fairly continuous or alternate with periods of depression. Furthermore, it can range from mild hypomania, which is seen in many energetic, well-functioning people, to psychotic mania that completely disrupts normal functioning.

DISTINCTION BETWEEN NEUROTIC AND PSYCHOTIC DEPRESSION

The distinction between neurotic and psychotic depression is not always easy to make, particularly in cases of severe neurotic depression. Neurotic (reactive) depression involves a real loss and therefore has a specific precipitant, but it is not always readily identifiable. Psychotic (endogenous) depression, on the other hand, may or may not, have a specific precipitant. Furthermore, there can be severe physiological reactions in both neurotic and psychotic depression. The main differences between the two are the degree of impaired functioning and the quality of self-reproaches. Though the neurotically depressed individual might be immobilized for a period of time by his loss, he will not display the confusion and disorientation of the psychotically depressed individual. Furthermore, in neurotic depression the self-reproaches may be extreme and quite unreasonable (e.g., a neurotically depressed teenage girl feels responsible for the car accident that killed her brother, even though she wasn't the driver, because she believes the accident would have been avoided if only she had asked the driver to stop at a restroom, as she had considered doing). However, the self-reproaches in neurotic depression are never as totally irrational and bizarre as in a psychotic depression (e.g., crying and muttering about Jesus Christ and polishing shoes).

ETIOLOGY OF DEPRESSION:
PSYCHOLOGICAL VS. ORGANIC FACTORS

The etiology of depression has been variously attributed to:

1. Psychological factors—the tendency to become depressed arises from early frustrations in the oral stage.

2. Organic factors—the tendency to become depressed arises from a physiological imbalance, which may be inherited.

3. Both psychological and organic factors—the tendency to develop neurotic depression arises from the early oral deprivations, while psychotic depression is caused by physiological imbalances.

Although there is no conclusive evidence to support any of these views, the third view is now the most widely accepted. But regardless of whether or not physical or psychological factors cause depression, it is obvious that depression is manifested both physically and psychologically.

METHODS OF TREATING DEPRESSION

A combined supportive and insight psychotherapy is the treatment of choice for neurotic depression to help the patient work through his grief and to separate realistic sadness from unrealistic self-reproaches. At some point, it may also be helpful to encourage the patient to become more active to overcome the depression. Medication is needed only in extreme cases of neurotic depression to help mobilize the patient to work through his grief or to calm down agitation in an agitated depression.

Medication is the prime treatment in cases of psychotic depression, because these patients are too deeply immersed in their misery to be reached by psychotherapy alone. No amount of reasoning will convince them that their self-reproaches are not justified. No changes in environment or in activity level will affect a psychotic depression. However, once the medication begins to work and the depression is somewhat lifted, psychotherapy can be useful to help the patient arrive at a more reasonable view of himself. ECT (shock therapy) is the most drastic, risky treatment of depression. It should not be used except as a last resort in the most extreme cases of depression which have proven resistant to all other forms of treatment. It certainly should not be used routinely.

What follows is a case of severe neurotic depression which at times reached psychotic proportions. For three months the patient was being treated with medication and psychoanalytic therapy aimed at helping him understand the source of his depression, without any success. The turning point in treatment came when the traditional psychoanalytic question of "Why?" was changed to the more existential question of "Why Not?"

CASE REPORT OF A DEPRESSED PATIENT

The patient, an unmarried professional in his midtwenties, entered a severe depression when he and his girlfriend broke up. To the patient, the dissolution of this relationship meant not only the loss of love, but also proof of his inadequacy as a male. The patient didn't date till he was close to 20 and he had feared that his late start meant he would never completely fill the "normal" male role. As a result he viewed each relationship with a female as a test of his adequacy as a male. This most recent relationship was the longest and most promising one he had ever had, and the loss of it convinced him that his original fears were well founded. He wanted very much to find another girlfriend, but he felt hopeless about ever establishing a lasting relationship. Before long he began feeling he couldn't even start a relationship, even if he tried. He considered himself totally lacking in any qualities a woman would want in a boyfriend.

His self-denigration soon spread to other areas of his life. He decided no one would want him as a friend. He felt he couldn't carry on a reasonable conversation. As a result, he started avoiding the people he knew and cared about to spare them the unpleasantness of his company. He also decided that he was making no real contribution at work, and that as soon as his colleagues realized it, he would be fired. But he wasn't going to wait till then. If he didn't improve by that summer, he would quit his profession and take a factory job somewhere away from everyone he knew.

After a while he became convinced he would never improve. His memory was rapidly deteriorating and he figured he had a brain tumor. Now he was only waiting for death, which he hoped would come soon. He wished he had the courage to end his life, and he considered his failure to do so further proof of his worthlessness.

For three months the depression persisted while the therapist sympathetically listened to all the patient's self-reproaches, asked questions about his present and past life to determine why he was making them, and reflected upon and interpreted his remarks. Insight into his relationship with his mother, whom he perceived as cold and rejecting, did not alter his feelings of worthlessness; nor did the therapist's pointing out how unreasonable his self-reproaches were. Finally the therapist decided a new tactic was necessary, and said to the patient: "You know, most people hate being depressed and try to fight it off. Why aren't you trying to fight it off?" The patient explained that he felt as if he were lying in a heap at the bottom of a steep wall which he had to scale to become a "normal, healthy" male. He could pick himself up and try to scale the wall, but he knew he'd keep falling down. So why even try? He figured it was better to stay at the bottom of the wall and accept his inadequacies than to keep trying and being disappointed.

The therapist then said: "To hear you talk about yourself, you sound like the lowest thing on earth. That's ridiculous. I know you feel all the terrible things you're saying, but I also believe that deep down you really know they aren't true and that you do have some wonderful qualities." The patient replied: "Sure, I know there are some flowers, but they're surrounded by weeds." The therapist responded: "So what? Everyone has weeds mixed in with their flowers." The patient then said: "But my weeds are much worse than other people's weeds." When the therapist asked what was so terrible about his weeds, he divulged his deepest fears. He worried about becoming an alcoholic because he drank heavily and his uncle was an alcoholic. He also worried about becoming a homosexual because he felt like such a failure as a heterosexual and he'd had some homosexual experiences when he was young. At this point the therapy hour was just about over; the therapist said that those were important issues and they should be discussed at the next session.

The next week the patient called to cancel his appointment because he had to cover for an absent colleague. At the same time he expressed annoyance at having to miss the session because this was the first time he had ever looked forward to the therapy hour. The following week when he was seen, the patient looked less depressed than he had been looking and he expressed some hopefulness that therapy was finally going to work. He then launched into a discussion of his deepest fears. After listening to him for a while, the therapist said that in view of his history, both of his fears were possible, but that didn't mean they necessarily had to come true. In both cases the choice was really up to him. These things are not decided by fate.

Those words had a striking effect on the patient. Whereas he previously had never accepted the therapist's attempts to soften his self-reproaches, he immediately accepted this line of reasoning about his deepest fears and he became very hopeful that therapy could help him eventually lead the "normal, healthy" life he so desired. From then on the patient's self-reproaches ceased entirely.

However this does not mean that his depression was over. It continued, but in a different, milder form, for several months. The main difference was that the patient was now preoccupied with his fear of death instead of his previous longing for death, and he didn't want to start really living until he could figure out the meaning of life and death. After discussing these issues in depth on a personal and philosophical level, the patient reached two conclusions. One was that he was wasting his life while he was pursuing its meaning, and even if he discovered the absolute true meaning (if there is such a thing), there would be no way of knowing for a certainty that he was right. Realizing all this, the patient decided he was tired of searching out the meaning of life and death and he wanted to start enjoying life again. He began socializing with his old friends and making new friends, including a new girlfriend. Moreover, he discovered to his amazement and delight that his memory had returned and that he could think of interesting things to talk about. He even discovered that he wasn't such a bad worker. In fact he was making some real contributions, even though he wasn't accomplishing all that he thought he should. But now he could see how hard he was on himself and how impossibly high his standards were. He decided he would continue striving for his goals, but he would try not to take each setback as a sign of utter failure and proof of his worthlessness.

After feeling really good about himself for two months, the patient decided to stop taking medication to see if he would feel good without drugs. When he noticed no decline in his mood, he started talking about terminating treatment. The therapy sessions were phased out over the next two months, during which time he continued to be in very good spirits.

Chapter 5

NEUROSIS

SYMPTOM AND CHARACTER NEUROSIS

A neurosis is a psychological dysfunction based on inner tension and conflict. Anxiety and depression, the most common neuroses, are reactions to stress that occur in all personality types. They are discussed in separate chapters. This chapter deals with character neuroses and their associated symptom neuroses.

Freud developed psychoanalysis as a method for treating symptom neuroses: anxiety neurosis (phobias); obsessive-compulsive neurosis (obsessive thoughts, compulsive rituals); hysterical neurosis (motor paralysis, sensory anesthesia). Freud showed that neurotic symptoms represent compromises between impulses and defenses and thereby exquisitely express inner conflict while keeping the individual unaware of it. Psychoanalysis was designed to uncover and resolve the unconscious conflict underlying the symptoms.

Symptom neuroses are not as common today as in Freud's time. The modern clinician is more likely to be confronted with character neuroses: obsessive-compulsive personalities and hysterical personalities whose neuroses pervade the whole personality and are not restricted to specific symptoms. Though persons with character neuroses may have some symptoms, their symptoms are rarely as dramatic in onset or intensity as the symptoms of Freud's patients. They are more likely to be subtle symptoms woven into the whole personality. Therefore the typical neurotic patient of today does not come for treatment to remove symptoms, but rather to improve his whole manner of functioning. The exception to this general observation is the still-prevalent phobic patient who seeks treatment to get rid of her phobia.

PHOBIAS

According to psychoanalytic theory, a phobia is fear displaced from a conflict-ridden object or situation to a neutral object or situation. Thus a small boy's phobia about animals might represent his fear of his father, which he finds too threatening to recognize because it stems from his own ambivalent feelings toward his father. A woman's phobia about going outside her home might represent a fear of sexual temptation which is especially threatening because she is not sexually fulfilled at home.

Phobias are common in children between the anal and phallic psychosexual levels of development (about three to five years). Adults who develop phobias are considered fixated at or regressed to that psychosexual level. Analysis, aimed at uncovering and resolving the original fear underlying the phobia, is a very lengthy method of treatment which is usually unnecessary.

Behavior therapy is the simplest, fastest, and most effective method for treating phobias. According to behavior theory, the neurosis is nothing more than the symptom, and therefore there is no need to uncover so-called unconscious conflicts. The symptom is attached directly by a deconditioning process called *systematic desensitization.* First the therapist records the hierarchy of the patient's fears associated with the particular phobia. The therapist also teaches the patient how to relax by successively tightening and relaxing every muscle of the body and taking deep breaths. Then the therapist leads the patient in fantasy or real life through his hierarchy of fears, starting with the least threatening situation and moving progressively to more threatening ones until the phobia is mastered. At each step of the hierarchy the patient practices the relaxation exercise and does not move on to the next step until she is completely relaxed.

CASE REPORT OF A PHOBIC PATIENT

Mrs. A, a 40-year-old mother of four, sought treatment for her avoidance of driving and riding in a car because of her fear of being in an accident. This phobia was causing her and her family a great deal of inconvenience and stress.

Therapy began in the traditional psychoanalytic manner of exploring the roots of Mrs. A's phobia. The previous summer the A family took a two-week driving vacation through many states. Mrs. A had been apprehensive about the long car ride and the behavior of her children. To her great relief, everything went well, but immediately after the trip she developed her phobia. Over the years her husband had described to her all the accidents he had seen in the course of his work as a truck driver, and she felt that these descriptions contributed to her phobia. However she did not understand why she developed the phobia after the long trip and not before. The therapist explained that many people are strong during a crisis, and that only after the crisis has passed do they let out their upset feelings. Evidently the long trip was more stressful to her than she had realized at the time.

Mrs. A indicated that she had always been a nervous individual, but her nervousness had increased greatly in the last two and a half years, since the arrival of her fourth child. She had been looking forward to the free time she would have once her third child entered school, and she was not too keen on starting over again with a new baby. To make matters worse, this child turned out to be hyperactive and far more difficult to manage than any of her other children. Mrs. A also mentioned that certain habits of her husband made her nervous and his impatience with her phobia was not helping matters.

At this point the therapist suggested that Mr. A join Mrs. A in the session to work on improving their relationship and the management of their youngest child, in the hope that Mrs. A's phobia would gradually subside as her general tension level was reduced. Mrs. A liked the idea and Mr. A readily agreed to cooperate. Thus began a very productive phase of therapy, during which many issues were resolved between the A's and the care of their youngest child became less of a strain on Mrs. A. Mrs. A was feeling much happier than before, and her phobia had subsided to the point where she could ride in a car without too much tension. However she was still unable to drive a car.

At this stage of Mrs. A's treatment, five months after her first visit, the therapist suggested that a behavior therapist be called in to attack the phobia directly through a conditioning process. Mrs. A would pay the behavior therapist the fee she had been paying the original therapist, who would attend the sessions to learn the technique. Mrs. A agreed to this plan and the behavior therapist was called in.

The first thing the behavior therapist* did was to list with Mrs. A all the possible situations she might encounter with a car—driving in heavy traffic, driving in a driveway, standing by a car, starting the motor, driving around the block, and so on. Then he had Mrs. A rate on a scale from 1 to 100 her degree of discomfort in each of the situations. Then the therapist rank-ordered all these situations according to Mrs. A's ratings.

Before proceeding through this hierarchy, the therapist taught Mrs. A a relaxation exercise. He directed her to tighten the muscles of her brow as much as she could and then slowly to relax them. After that he directed her to tighten the muscles around her eyes and then slowly relax them. In this manner Mrs. A tightened and relaxed all the muscles of her body. At the end of the exercise she was instructed to take a deep sigh. Mrs. A said this exercise was so relaxing, she almost felt like she was floating. She was instructed to do this twice a day for the next week.

At the next session, after it was determined that Mrs. A had mastered the relaxation exercise, she was given the first set of instructions for desensitization. She was told to stand by her car two times a day for 15 minutes. If she became anxious, she should do her relaxation exercise.

At each subsequent session, the previous week's exercise was discussed. If it was completed successfully, Mrs. A was instructed to go to the next step in her hierarchy. It not, she was to repeat the step until she had mastered it without any anxiety. By the end of the tenth session Mrs. A was driving without any anxiety on streets with little traffic. By taking roundabout routes to avoid heavy traffic, she was able to do all the driving she found necessary as a housewife and mother. At this point Mrs. A decided to terminate treatment because she was completely satisfied with the results thus far and she had no desire to drive in heavy traffic.

* Peter A. Wish, Ph.D., Executive Director of the New England Institute of Human Sexuality. Framingham, Massachusetts.

HYSTERICAL NEUROSIS

The hysterical (neurotic character) is an overly emotional, impulsive individual who avoids thinking about motivation and the consequences of behavior. Repression is the major defense. According to psychoanalytic theory, hysterical personalities are unable to resolve their Oedipal/Electra complex (sometimes between four and six years of age). As a result they are fixated at the phallic stage of psychosexual development and are very conflicted over sexual impulses. Typically, hysterics express this conflict by repressing sexual feelings in situations that normally evoke sexuality and displaying sexual feelings in situations that are not normally considered sexual, all the time totally unaware of what they are doing. In addition, hysterics may act out in their lives a re-creation of their Oedipal/Electra complex (e.g., by being sexually attracted only to persons resembling the opposite-sex parent or by seeking sexual relationships only with persons who are already married).

CASE REPORT OF AN HYSTERICAL PATIENT

L, a 26-year-old woman, sought treatment to straighten out her life. L's childhood feeling of security had been shattered by and was never restored after her father's sudden death when she was only eight. After her father's death, L and her mother and older sister moved frequently from city to city, staying with different relatives, sometimes not even together. In addition, L doubted whether her mother and sister really loved her, so involved were they with their own lives.

L was very bright in school, but she dropped out after her junior year in high school because of an illegitimate pregnancy. L wanted to keep the baby, but when the baby's father refused to provide a home, she decided it would be best for the baby to give it up for adoption. Afterwards, her boyfriend agreed to marry her. Though she could not really forgive him for not wanting their baby, L was so eager for love she was glad that at least he wanted her. The marriage proved to be unhappy and made L doubt whether her husband had ever really loved her. After a couple of years she sued for divorce.

After her divorce, L acquired a high school equivalency degree and worked at a number of short-lived, unskilled office jobs. L would invariably antagonize everyone by making numerous suggestions for improving office procedure. She thought she was only trying to be helpful and win friends, and therefore it was difficult for .L to understand what went wrong.

L had little difficulty starting romantic relationships, and she began many, because all she asked for in a man was that he show some interest in her. L gave a lot to these relationships and she could not understand why they would invariably fizzle out.

L was interested in group therapy for two reasons. She had had extensive individual therapy in the past and she wanted to try group therapy for a change. Moreover, she wanted feedback from many people to help her figure out what was going wrong in her relationships. Accordingly, L was assigned to a newly formed therapy group.

She proved to be the most active member of the group in discussing her own problems and in responding to the problems of others. Although she tended to dominate the group to a great extent, no one resented her because she was very giving, as well as demanding of attention. Moreover, her liveliness and openness helped loosen things up and made the other group members feel more comfortable about discussing their problems.

L received much sympathy from group members for her difficulties with men, plus assurance that she was worthy of a lasting relationship. In time it became apparent that L's extreme eagerness for a relationship was largely responsible for her repeated disappointments. She was like an ice skater eagerly rushing onto a pond to skate, without testing whether the ice was strong enough to support her; as a result she would invariably fall through. L could see this and could understand that she would have to become more cautious before she could establish a secure, lasting relationship.

Understanding the problem, however, did not immediately bring about a solution. It took many months before L learned to be more selective and to proceed slowly in developing relationships. During this time the group gave L the emotional support she needed to overcome the desperate feelings that had promoted her self-defeating behavior. At the same time L worked on her difficulty in keeping a job, which paralleled her difficulty in keeping a boyfriend. She learned to delay her impulses and to imagine their possible effect on other people before deciding whether or not to act on them.

After two and a half years of treatment, L felt ready to leave group, a much happier person than when she entered. She was still a lively, emotionally expressive individual, but she was more cautious than before. She was more tuned into other people's feelings and as a result was much better able to protect herself from being hurt. Finally, she was engaged to marry a dependable man and she found a job that utilized her skills.

OBSESSIVE-COMPULSIVE NEUROSIS

The obsessive-compulsive neurotic character is an overly intellectualized, rigidly compulsive individual who has lost touch with her deep feelings. Intellectualization, isolation of affect, and reaction formation are the major defenses. According to psychoanalytic theory, the obsessive-compulsive did not adequately deal with toilet training and autonomy issues (between the ages of one and one-half and three.) As a result, the obsessive-compulsive is fixated at the anal stage of psychosexual development and is full of conflict about impulses to be dirty, messy, disorderly, and aggressive.

Typically, the obsessive-compulsive defends herself against these impulses with a reaction formation of being superclean, neat, orderly, and unaggressive. However, this may not be enough to keep the unacceptable impulses out of awareness. For example, an obsessive-compulsive may be bothered by aggressive thoughts that suddenly, and for no apparent reason, pop into her mind. Since the obsessive-compulsive successfully isolates her feelings and is therefore unaware of her anger, she views these aggressive thoughts as not belonging to herself (i.e., ego-dystonic). To avoid feeling anxious, an obsessive-compulsive may feel compelled to perform certain rituals—like checking the gas on the stove several times before leaving the house, or praying for a prescribed length of time. Usually the obsessive-compulsive regards these rituals as very annoying, but feels unable to cease performing them.

Psychoanalytic treatment of obsessive-compulsive patients is aimed at making the unconscious conflicts conscious and thereby removing the impetus for the obsessive-compulsive symptom. This is more easily said than done because in contrast to the pliable, suggestible hysterical patient, the obsessive-compulsive's favorite defense of intellectualization often makes it seem that more is being accomplished in analytic treatment than actually is. The obsessive-compulsive is able to make intricate analyses of her behavior and to develop brilliant insights, which nonetheless do not affect her emotionally. Thus psychoanalytic therapy can be misused by obsessive-compulsives to maintain their neurosis instead of curing it. It is for these reasons that other forms of treatment are often more effective in breaking through the obsessive-compulsive's intellectualizing defenses.

Gestalt therapy is ideally suited to obsessive-compulsive neurotic characters who live too much in their thoughts and need to get more in touch with their feelings. Whereas the analytic therapies focus on understanding past experiences, Gestalt therapy focuses on immediate awareness of present experiences. Whereas analytic patients free associate to dream images to uncover their unconscious meanings, Gestalt patients act out different parts of their dreams to experience their full emotional impact. While the analytic patient describes how she feels about a significant person in her life, the Gestalt patient imagines this person in the room and expresses her feelings to the person. It is obvious how all these techniques cut right through intellectualizing defenses to the patient's deepest feelings.

The behavior therapy technique of thought stopping is ideally suited to the control of obsessive thinking. The patient is told to tell herself "stop" everytime an obsessive thought comes to mind. The first day she might have to tell herself "stop" 100 times, but the next day it will be much less, and in a few days she will hardly have to say it at all.

The following case study describes an obsessive-compulsive personality who was treated in short-term treatment (seven sessions) with a combination of behavior and Gestalt techniques.

CASE REPORT OF AN OBSESSIVE-COMPULSIVE PATIENT

S was a 23-year-old graduate student who sought treatment two months before finishing school and moving out of the state. She wanted help to overcome her conflict and anxiety concerning her relationship with her boyfriend. She had become seriously involved with a young man from a different religious and social background. He was a fine person, he shared S's values, and he was willing to convert to her religion. Nevertheless, S obsessed over the advisability of continuing the relationship. If she wasn't going to end up marrying him, she felt it was best for them to end the relationship right away so she wouldn't be wasting time finding a suitable husband. Her parents seemed to accept her boyfriend, but she worried that they were secretly displeased with him and wouldn't love him as much as they loved her brother's wife. S's boyfriend had returned to college to take courses necessary for entering a graduate program, but S worried that he might not be accepted into graduate school. She respected his intelligence, but she felt his poorer social background limited him so that he was not as socially adept or articulate as she would like him to be. S discussed these concerns incessantly with her girlfriends, her mother, and even her boyfriend. When there was no one available with whom she could discuss her concerns, she would go over and over them in her mind.

After hearing about all S's concerns, the therapist asked her whether she loved her boyfriend. S said she didn't know for sure. She thought she must care for him a lot because she traveled a long distance to visit him on weekends. But she wasn't sure if she actually loved him. The therapist suggested it would be important to find out whether she loved him before she made any decision about continuing the relationship. S agreed, but didn't know how she could go about finding out for sure. Her obsessive worries prevented her from discovering her true feelings.

As a first step toward overcoming her anxiety about the relationship, the therapist recommended that S stop talking about it to everyone except the therapist. At the next session S reported feeling somewhat less anxious since she stopped discussing her concerns with everyone. However she was still bothered by her own obsessive thoughts on the subject. Accordingly the therapist demonstrated the thought stopping technique and recommended she use it whenever she thought about the relationship outside the therapy hour. The following session S reported feeling even better than the week before now that she had stopped her continual obsessing.

S spent the next few therapy sessions analyzing her feelings about her boyfriend, but she was no closer to knowing whether he was the right person for her or even if she loved him. When the therapist asked S how she felt when she was with him, she said she couldn't say. All she could remember was her worrying about the future. Accordingly, the therapist recommended that at their next meeting she push all thoughts of the future from her mind (by thought stopping) and instead notice her physical and emotional reactions to him, particularly upon seeing him after a long separation.

At the very next session S reported many strong positive feelings that she had noticed when she was with her boyfriend and she firmly concluded that she really did love him. S's certainty that she loved him dispelled most of her anxieties about whether her parents would love him. She decided it was more important that she love him than for her parents to love him; as long as they accepted him, she wouldn't have any problems from them. Her certainty about loving him also diminished many of her concerns about what she perceived to be her boyfriend's social shortcomings. She decided his shortcomings were not so terrible and did not outweigh her love for him.

After analyzing and resolving all these doubts, S was left with two concerns—whether her boyfriend would get into graduate school and what would happen if he did not. She now knew that she wanted to marry him, but she feared that the relationship would fall apart if he could not reach her level of achievement. At this point the therapist suggested that in view of the fact that she loved him and wanted to marry him, all she could do was wait and hope for the best. Within a year she would know either way. Since she did love him he certainly was worth the investment of her time, which after all wasn't so great. If they did break up she would still be young and still have other chances to get married. In the meantime she could concentrate on enjoying the relationship and not get bogged down by worrying about the future.

S readily agreed with these recommendations and tried very hard to carry them out. All her friends commented on how much more relaxed she was and she herself reported feeling much much better. Treatment ended as planned when S finished graduate school and moved out of state.

Chapter 6

PERSONALITY AND CHARACTER DISORDERS

Personality and character disorders refer to socially mal-adaptive behavior which is ego-syntonic. In other words, the individual is unhappy only when conflicts with others jeopardize the fulfillment of his needs. Although the terms personality and character disorders are generally used interchangeable, it is the author's opinion that the former should be reserved for overly passive behavior in which the individual tries to manipulate the environment through passivity and that the latter should refer only to overly active behavior in which the individual tries to manipulate the environment through activity. Moreover, those personality and character disorders that are so severe as to be nearly psychotic should be classified as borderline conditions.

PERSONALITY DISORDERS

- The passive-dependent personality manipulates others to satisfy his extreme dependency needs through overly passive behavior.

- The passive-aggressive personality is too passive to express anger openly, so he expresses it in subtle, indirect ways, often without fully realizing it.
- The masochistic personality welcomes abuse in relationships and enjoys the role of "victim."
- The immature personality has no serious distortions in his personality, but characteristically functions at an immature level of development.
- The inadequate personality can't cope with life's demands, and functioning is seriously impaired in all areas.

Character Disorders

- The explosive personality is usually passive, but occasionally has intense, uncontrollable outbursts of rage which he later regrets.
- The impulse-ridden character's behavior is dominated by impulses without any thought about the consequences.
- The alcoholic personality lets alcohol dominate his life at the expense of other satisfactions.
- The drug-dependent personality allows drugs to dominate his life at the expense of other satisfactions.
- The antisocial personality repeatedly engages in antisocial behavior for little or no reason, is incapable of real attachment or loyalty, and is unable to feel guilt.
- The sexual pervert's behavior is dominated by overwhelming, bizarre sexual urges, because he cannot achieve sexual satisfaction in conventional ways.

The narcissistic (extremely self-centered) personality lies somewhere between personality disorders and character disorders. At times the narcissistic personality manipulates the environment through passivity and at other times through activity.

BORDERLINE CONDITIONS

- The schizoid personality is extremely withdrawn from others and detached from his own emotions. His major satisfactions in life come from fantasies, but unlike a true psychotic, he can distinguish fantasy from reality.
- The paranoid personality is overly suspicious of others and has an overly important view of himself.
- The cyclothymic personality experiences extreme shifts in mood unrelated to external events.
- The borderline personality is characterized by severely weakened ego identity, judgment, and reality sense without a formal thought disorder; he has multiple neurotic, personality, and character disorder symptoms.

ETIOLOGY OF PERSONALITY AND CHARACTER DISORDERS

Despite differences in overt behavior, the etiology and treatment of personality and character disorders have much in common. Chronic low self-esteem and low self-confidence seem to underly both the personality and character disorders. However, instead of feeling neurotically depressed about their felt inadequacies, these individuals develop behavior patterns that defend them against fully experiencing the pain of their low self-esteem and low self-confidence. People with personality disorders behave passively to avoid competition and criticism, and when things go wrong they blame the outside world, while people with character disorders throw themselves into activities that reduce painful awareness of their inadequacies.

TREATING PERSONALITY AND CHARACTER DISORDERS

The first step in treating personality and character disorders is to establish a therapeutic relationship in which the therapist demonstrates a feeling of genuine concern for the patient. This entails more than a philosophical acceptance of the patient as an individual of worth and faith in his potential simply because he is a human being. Individuals with personality and character disorders are extremely defensive about their personal failings; they need to feel liked by the therapist before they can begin to look at their shortcomings.

Of course it may not always be easy for a therapist to like a patient. However it should be remembered that liking a person is not the same thing as approving of all that person's behavior. What the therapist must convey is a feeling of liking the patient, despite his faults. Then the therapist must help the patient see how his socially undesirable behavior hurts himself even more than it hurts others. In this way the therapist shows he is on the patient's side and has the best interests of the patient in mind. If the therapist cannot find at least one thing to like in the patient that could be a cornerstone of the therapeutic relationship, it is best to transfer that patient to another therapist who could develop a therapeutic relationship with the patient.

Once a therapeutic relationship is established and the patient can begin to look at his behavior and its harmful effects, it is important to help the patient understand how he developed this behavior. This understanding may make the unpleasant facts of his behavior less painful, but it should not be used as an excuse or justification for the behavior. On the contrary; the understanding should be used to help the patient gain control over his behavior and become more responsible.

In some cases an understanding of the causes and effects of the undesirable behavior is sufficient impetus for the patient to start changing his behavior. But in many cases, although the patient wishes to change, he does not know how to go about making the changes. In these cases practical guidance from the therapist is needed before the patient can make these changes. With personality disorders the guidance will consist of suggesting ways the patient can assert himself more and develop greater independence. With character disorders the guidance will consist of suggesting ways in which the patient can find more socially acceptable ways of gratifying his needs.

The following is a case of an impulse-ridden character.

CASE REPORT OF AN IMPULSE RIDDEN CHARACTER DISORDER

J was a 26-year-old, unmarried, gay, welfare mother with a history of drug abuse and alcoholism. Her childhood had been very unhappy because she felt her mother had a cruel, unfeeling attitude toward her. She entered therapy after nine months of steady contact with a telephone hot line service. During that time J managed to stop taking drugs, but she was still drinking very heavily. She was very fearful about starting treatment and said practically nothing the first session. During the following week she took an overdose of sleeping pills and ended up in a hospital emergency room where her stomach was pumped.

When the therapist learned about this at the next session, the therapist asked J why she did it. J said she was very upset and didn't know what else to do. She adamantly denied wanting to kill herself. She said she had too much to live for, primarily her son. The therapist then told J to phone her the next time she felt that way so she could talk over whatever was upsetting her instead of taking an overdose. J took the therapist's home phone number and thanked her for it.

But the next week she took another overdose of sleeping pills. At the next session J explained the event exactly as before and said jokingly that the emergency room staff must be very tired of her. The therapist reminded J of her agreement to phone if she felt that way again and told J that she couldn't keep behaving in this way. Someday she could finish by killing herself, without really meaning to. If she took another overdose, the therapist said she would have to arrange psychiatric hospitalization for her. J then said she couldn't go to a hospital and leave her son. The therapist said she should think of that the next time she felt like taking an overdose; instead she should call the therapist to talk about her feelings.

After this discussion J did not have a recurrence of her urge to take an overdose. However she did take to phoning the therapist at home after each session to tell the therapist what she had been too inhibited to say face to face. The therapist permitted these calls as a way of building up a therapeutic relationship, but after a while, when the therapist felt she had proven her interest in and desire to help J, the therapist told J that the time had come to stop the calls. From then on she would have to speak her mind during the session or wait till the next session. J could phone the therapist only in an emergency.

Considering J's explosive nature, she took this limit setting very well. She agreed it was entirely reasonable and said that she knew it wasn't fair to take up the therapist's time at home. From then on J restricted her phone calls to infrequent occasions when she was extremely upset.

The major source of J's upsets were her fights with her lover. In these fights J could be very cruel in what she said, as well as violent in her actions. Moreover, she did not display any guilt about these episodes. The therapist would tell J that no matter how much she hurt other people, she was hurting herself most of all, because she couldn't help feeling bad about herself.

J admitted that her behavior made her feel that she was a rotten person and agreed that she should control her temper for her own sake, as well as for others. But this was more easily said than done. While J stopped being physically violent, she continued to express her aggression verbally with much cruelty. At one point the therapist told J that she was like a beautiful, wild stallion with a lot of wonderful things in her, but needing to be tamed. J loved this image of herself and told the therapist she wanted to be tamed in therapy, to be more civilized.

About two months after treatment began, J came to a session with a woman from the telephone hot line who wanted to speak to the therapist about J's excessive drinking. This woman insisted that the therapist had to stop J from drinking because J was damaging her health. The therapist agreed that it was a good idea for J to stop drinking, but that she, the therapist, had no magic power to make J suddenly stop. It was up to J to want to stop. All the therapist could do was help J find other satisfactions in life so she wouldn't need to drink so much.

From then on the therapist actively encouraged J to socialize with her neighbors to occupy her time so she wouldn't be sitting alone in her apartment all day drinking from boredom and loneliness. J could see the sense in this suggestion and admitted that she was lonely while her son was at school. However she said she felt timid about socializing with new people. The therapist pointed out the contradiction between her extreme outspokenness with people she knew and her shyness with new people. J then said she was afraid of being rejected by someone new. The therapist pointed out that J was so bright and so much fun that her lover never rejected her, no matter how difficult she was. Therefore, if J just acted halfway nice, she would have no trouble making new friends. With this support, J started reaching out to some neighbors, and in a short time she was spending a lot of time with one neighbor. As the therapist predicted, she also began drinking less and less.

As a result of her increased socialization and her reduced drinking, J began to feel quite pleased with her progress and eager to make even more progress. Then a very traumatic event occurred. After an unpleasant scene with her parents in which J loudly complained about the cheapness of their birthday gift for her son, J received a letter from her mother denouncing her unacceptable behavior over the years and severing their relationship for all time. This letter stunned J. Though she had always felt emotionally rejected by her mother, she had never expected such an extreme repudiation of herself. J cried and cried about this, but did nothing to retaliate even though she could have told her mother a secret that she believed would have destroyed her mother. The therapist pointed out that no matter how she had hurt people in the past, she never actually destroyed anyone, and here she had the provocation and the opportunity to destroy someone, but did not. Therefore, deep down, she must really be a decent person. This new view of herself gave J much needed strength to cope with the hurt she was experiencing. It also gave her an incentive to prove even further that she could be a good person.

However J was soon faced with another trauma. Welfare sent her a letter stating that all welfare mothers with school-age children must enroll in a job training program. This upset J exceedingly. She didn't want to be away when her son returned from school. The therapist said that wasn't necessarily a bad thing. Since her son was an only child with a single parent, it would probably be good for him to spend his afternoons with a family where he could learn the give-and-take of sibling relationships and have another adult to depend upon in addition to his mother. J readily agreed with this line of reasoning, but then raised other objections to her working. She said she was terrified of being out in the world. She had never worked before. She didn't think she could cope with all the pressures. She was afraid to be with groups of people.

The therapist pointed out that she was certainly bright enough to do very well in a job training program, and as for her fear of being with people, she had already proven she could make new friends. J said she didn't mind being with individual people, but groups of people frightened her.

At this point the therapist raised the possibility of J entering a therapy group led by the therapist. J was frightened, but the idea intrigued her. The next few sessions were devoted to preparing J for entry into the group. In addition to explaining the process of group therapy and answering J's questions about it, the therapist expressed concern that J might destructively lash out at a group member as she had done in the past with other people. The therapist reminded J that all the people in the group were hurting and that J should try to be helpful to them as they would be to her. Any confrontations should be motivated by a desire to help, not to hurt. J agreed to these conditions, though she was not so worried about her ability to hurt others as their possible rejection of her. Finally, after receiving a great deal of encouragement and support, J agreed on a date for entering the group.

Group therapy turned out to be an extremely positive experience for J. She was very quiet at first, but the group reached out to her. Encouraged, J started speaking up and telling about herself. The group found J's outspokeness very refreshing and everyone liked her tremendously. They also offered a great deal of emotional support whenever she was troubled by something. For many months J was very much on the receiving end of the group's attention and showed very little interest in giving to any other group member. In fact, whenever another group member dominated a session, she would express annoyance because she felt she didn't get enough time. When no one in the group confronted her with the fact that she usually dominated the sessions and it was only fair for someone else to have a turn, the therapist pointed this out. Later, at an individual session, the therapist pointed out to J how she saw people through a film of her own needs. Rarely did enough light get through for her to see people for themselves. J pondered this idea awhile, and though she didn't like it, she couldn't really deny it.

Soon afterwards, J became friendly with a very troubled neighbor. For the first time in her life, J assumed a giving, supportive role and found that she liked it. She even wrote a poem which she shared with the group, describing how in the past she could see people only in terms of what they could give her, but now she had discovered the joy of giving to others. From then on, J started demonstrating in the group that she was interested in giving as well as receiving.

J's individual and group therapy ended when the therapist left the clinic. J understood why the therapist left. Nevertheless, she angrily refused to be transferred to another therapist in the clinic for weekly sessions or to see the therapist privately for a half hour every other week for a token fee. Though the therapist felt badly that so much good work ended on such an angry note, the therapist felt hopeful that J would continue to utilize and build upon what she had gained in treatment.

A phone call by J to the therapist a year later confirmed the therapist's hopes. J wanted to let the therapist know how well she had done in the past year and to apologize for her angry parting. J said she had had an absolutely marvelous time in school the past year, making friends and learning bookkeeping. She had done so well that the school wanted to hire her to work in their office. J was very flattered by this offer, but she couldn't accept it because she had planned on moving to a friend's farm 50 miles away with a nearby industrial complex where she could find work. J was getting along better than ever with her lover and she was drinking very little. She was very pleased with all the progress she had made and felt really good about herself.

Chapter 7

BORDERLINE PERSONALITIES

CLINICAL DESCRIPTION

The hallmark of the borderline personality is a chronic, specific type of ego defect, similar to, but not as severe as the ego defect found in schizophrenia. There are disturbances in judgment, realistic planning, foreseeing consequences, and connecting cause and effect, but there is no formal thought disorder. The reality sense is impaired by the invasion of primary process thinking, but reality testing is intact. The ego boundaries are unstable and the ego identity is weak, but the individual never completely loses her identity. Transient psychotic episodes may occur under stress, but these are short-lived. In fact this type of patient shows remarkable stability in her instability. Though she may frequently zig-zag over the reality line, she never goes so far as to develop a full-blown psychosis. Accompanying this nearly psychotic ego defect is a wide array of neurotic and character disorder symptoms which are present in varying combinations. In fact it appears that the more severe and extensive the neurotic and character disorder symptomatology, the more likely there is an associated ego defect.

TREATING BORDERLINE PERSONALITIES

Psychoanalytic therapy suitable for inhibited neurotics who need to have their unconscious conflicts brought into consciousness is completely unsuitable for patients with severe ego defects. These patients need to have their primary process thinking and antisocial impulses removed from consciousness. Therefore treatment must be directed toward present reality and the strengthening of ego controls. To heighten the ego functions of judgment, forethought, and impulse control, the therapist should help the patient see how present difficulties arose out of the past and also to learn better ways of handling troublesome situations. Ego identity can be strengthened in many ways. Ego boundaries can be established by bringing interpersonal relations more sharply into focus and by helping the patient distinguish herself more clearly from others. Historical continuity of the ego identity can be promoted by reminding the patient of her changeable moods. Positive ego identity can be enhanced through identification with a therapist who is a friendly, active, real person to the patient. One way to accomplish this is for the therapist to answer the patient's questions directly instead of interpreting them or reflecting them back. Two additional merits of this procedure are that it provides the patient with information needed for her growth and it keeps the patient focused on reality instead of fantasy.

CASE REPORTS OF TWO STRIKINGLY SIMILAR
BORDERLINE PATIENTS

In both cases there was a history of parental alcoholism, paternal seductiveness, running away from home in adolescence, and unwilling submission to homosexual advances.

Mrs. B. felt her parents encouraged her and her two brothers to drink heavily. As a child Mrs. B received little attention from her father, but once she reached puberty she became "his drinking buddy," "the apple of his eye." Beginning with her twelfth birthday her father began his yearly custom of taking her to his favorite bar so the two of them could celebrate their joint birthday. On these occasions, as well as at other times, her father would dance with her and encourage her to dance and flirt with his friends. After she was married, her father would go to her house whenever he was drunk to talk to her.

While in high school Mrs. B's best friend was a girl one year older than herself who had a reputation for wild behavior. Mrs. B idolized this friend so much that she followed her lead in everything, including traveling 1000 miles away from home even though she had no particular reason to do so. This friend introduced her to sex by demonstrating techniques on her. Although Mrs. B felt unwilling to take part in these activities, she could never say no to her friend, and so these relations continued on and off for many years, with Mrs. B's friend always taking the active role. Mrs. B saw her friend as a mother figure who was always there and always thought she was adorable.

Miss C's father was overtly seductive toward her as the oldest daughter in the family. In her early teens, when she started showing interest in boys, he began calling her a tramp. Once when he found her kissing a boy he flew into a rage and called her a prostitute. Later on, he made sexual advances to her, saying that since everyone else had a turn, why shouldn't he have one too.

After she ran away from home, Miss C's parents placed her in a reformatory. While there she was seduced on a few occasions by other girls. She found these experiences so upsetting that she would abruptly stop them. In her early twenties she had one more upsetting lesbian experience while under the influence of alcohol.

The major difference between Mrs. B and Miss C was the way they perceived their mothers. Mrs. B apparently saw her mother as a neutral figure because she said very little about her, either good or bad. Miss C, on the other hand, repeatedly discussed her hurt and confusion over her mother's extreme and contradictory sexual standards. For years her mother preached sexual chastity. Then when Miss C was around 17 years of age, her mother started having sexual relations with boys Miss C's age. Miss C's mother also let her know that she had been conceived out of wedlock.

Symptomatology

Mrs. B and Miss C exhibited the same cyclical pattern of behavior: anxiety and social withdrawal, excessive drinking, sexual promiscuity, guilt and depression, anxiety and social withdrawal, etc. In their anxious phase they would seclude themselves at home because they felt too self-conscious and inadequate to socialize with anyone outside their home. Mrs. B was so dependent on her extremely accepting and supportive husband that although she had many complaints against him, she knew she could never leave him unless she found another man on whom she could similarly depend. Miss C was also extremely dependent on her boyfriend for his fairly constant companionship, even though he treated her badly on a number of occassions.

When they were alone, Mrs. B and Miss C would worry about the possibility that deep down they desired lesbian and incestuous relations, however much these ideas consciously repelled them. Miss C also worried about her aggressively tinged sexual fantasies.

At times their tensions would erupt into acute somatic reactions that made them feel they were dying or going crazy. Mrs. B would have the feeling that her hands and feet were not part of her, or else she would feel numb all over. Miss C would have rapid heartbeat and shortness of breath. Sometimes they would hallucinate during these attacks. Mrs. B would see a flashing light. Miss C would see a hand coming toward her. In one attack Miss C had a delusion that she had killed her daughter.

When their tensions became unbearable, they would seek release through drinking and sex. Alcohol would relieve their anxiety and lift their social inhibitions. They would become lively, charming, and sexually free.

While her husband was working, Mrs. B would go with a girlfriend to a bar where they would drink and pick up men. Somehow Mrs. B always ended up in bed, although she could not recall how she got there and she did not remember having sexual relations. However the realization that she probably had filled her with shame and she never wanted to see the man again. The next day she would be overcome with intense feelings of guilt and depression. She blamed her loose sexual behavior on her drinking because she preferred to consider herself an "alcoholic" rather than a "tramp." Nevertheless, she recognized that her behavior was motivated in part by her wish to find her "knight in shining armor."

Miss C would go to bars by herself or with a girlfriend with the express purpose of getting drunk and finding a sexual partner. The next day she would be filled with loathing for herself and for the man whom she never wanted to see again. The main reason for her self-loathing was that she attained satisfaction only through oral relations, never through regular intercourse. This would make her feel perverted and she would start ruminating over her mother's accusations that she was to blame for her father's sexual advances toward her which caused the break-up of the marriage. Miss C did not want to believe this, but she felt it might be true. She remembered fantasizing sexual relations with her father when she was a child, and she wondered if perhaps he had detected this and that was why he made advances.

In time their depressed feelings would lift and their anxieties would begin to mount again, thereby starting a new cycle of acting out behavior.

Another thing Mrs. B and Miss C had in common was their inability to say no to anyone for any reason. It did not matter whether the person was a friend or a stranger, whether they liked the person or not. They simply could not turn anyone away for fear of hurting that person's feelings. As a result they frequently ended up hurting themselves. When anyone came to her door, Mrs. B would invite him in regardless of the hour, her mood, or her interest in him. Strange salesmen would leave her house patting her behind, and though she felt this was degrading, she could never express her annoyance. Miss C allowed her friends to take advantage of her over and over. She permitted her girlfriend to live in her apartment even after this friend had stolen some things from her. Her boyfriend's friends often patted her familiarly, and though this made her uncomfortable, she never knew how to stop them.

Evidently, Mrs. B and Miss C did not feel worthy enough to stand up for their rights and protect themselves. However the problem seems to go even deeper. It appears that they suffered not only from low self-esteem, but from a weak sense of their own identity. Whenever they received attention from a forceful person, their egos would fuse with the other person and they would be unable to distinguish what they wanted from what the other person wanted.

Therapy

The long-term individual therapist* for Mrs. B and Miss C assumed a faily active role in terms of offering a great deal of support to relieve anxiety and offering suggestions to increase control of distressing behavior. Interpretations were offered with the same aim of relieving anxiety and increasing control of upsetting behavior. These interpretations had the additional, unexpected effect of increasing the patients' faith in the therapist. The patients viewed them as indications that the therapist must really understand them, even though they did not understand themselves. This was a source of comfort to the patients and gave them hope that with the therapist's help their disturbing behavior could be changed. The course and management of therapy for Mrs. B and Miss C were similar. This section highlights some of the main therapeutic interventions and their effects.

Early in therapy, both Mrs. B and Miss C focused on their difficulty in saying no. Analysis of their feelings in situations in which they wanted to say no but couldn't showed that they were afraid they might hurt or anger the other person and end up being rejected themselves. In addition, there were times they just did not know why they could not say no, almost as if they had no will of their own. The therapist pointed out the choices they kept making, i.e., hurting and angering themselves rather than others, and self-dislike instead of possible rejection by others. The therapist questioned whether they were not worth at least as much as other people who made unpleasant demands on them. As for the times they did not know why they could not say no, the therapist pointed out that they allowed other people to dominate them so much that they did not even stop to think what was best for them. After much discussion, Mrs. B and Miss C began to accept the therapist's opinion that they were

---

*   Prior to long-term individual therapies, Mrs. B was in couples therapy and short-term individual therapy; Miss C was in group therapy.

worth something and that there was merit in thinking of themselves as well as of others. This new discovery pleased both patients enormously. However they had difficulty knowing how to implement it without creating the ill feelings they still feared. At this juncture patient and therapist role-played different situations, and both patients learned how to say no in a firm, yet friendly manner so as to minimize negative reactions. It was not long before they were carrying this out in their everyday lives and finding it was not as difficult as they had imagined.

As already indicated, Mrs. B blamed her sexual looseness on her excessive drinking because she preferred to consider herself an "alcoholic" rather than a "tramp." The therapist offered an entirely different view of her behavior. First of all, Mrs. B was not an alcoholic because she had control of her drinking. For that matter, she was unconsciously using liquor for the purpose of lifting her inhibitions and relieving herself of any responsibility for loose sexual behavior. On the other hand, this did not mean that she was a tramp. Her behavior was completely understandable in terms of certain deep psychological factors. Mrs. B's response to these interpretations was extremely positive. She expressed great relief at having finally found a therapist who understood her and therefore could help her change. Although she regretted giving up her "alcoholism" as a crutch to explain away her sexual looseness, she appreciated the fact that the therapist did not adopt her alternative view of herself as a "tramp." Moreover, she was intrigued with the idea of a psychological explanation for her behavior, and she was eager to find out what it was. To begin this process, the therapist related her present pattern of picking up men in bars to the time her father brought her to bars and encouraged her to flirt with his friends. She could see how her present behavior re-created the past, and she was fully aware of her craving for male attention. In this context she discussed her dissatisfactions with her husband and her search for someone better.

Sometime later, while discussing her close relationship with her father, the therapist suggested that Mrs. B's picking up men at different bars unconsciously symbolized a search for her father. While she was horrified at the idea that she might have an unconscious sexual desire for her father, she immediately confirmed this interpretation by relating two recent incidents. The first was that she became aroused while reading a story about an incestuous father-daughter relationship. The second was a dream in which she was having relations with her father. The therapist assured her that these impulses are universal, though normally unconscious. The problem in her case was.that her father's singling her out for special attention aroused these desires and kept her from completely repressing them. Since she knew she could never satisfy them directly, she sought their substitute gratification with men she met in bars. Glad of some explanation for her behavior, Mrs. B readily accepted these interpretations, though she did not fully understand them. This was soon evident because her acting out behavior continued as before.

About a month later when Mrs. B was complaining about her morning-after, guilty depression, the therapist suggested an experiment, namely, that she give up going to bars for a month to see how that made her feel. Willing to try anything to get rid of her terrible guilty depressions, she agreed to the experiment. Mrs. B managed to stay away from bars for the entire month, initially because of a cold and then through self-control. At the end of the month she reported feeling wonderful. In fact, she felt so good she decided to give up drinking altogether. A short while later she asked the therapist's opinion about her drinking in moderation at home or when she was out with her husband. The therapist reminded her that she was not an alcoholic and therefore she could drink in moderation if she chose. With this, Mrs. B resumed her drinking with several important differences. She stayed away from bars, and when she drank at home, she limited her drinking to beer.

Miss C also learned to control her drinking and sexual behavior, but in quite a different way. Miss C connected her feelings of worthlessness to her sexual looseness. However, much as she would have liked to be rid of her worthless feeling, she could see no alternative to her pattern of sexual promiscuity. She needed sex; besides, she was not so sure it was wrong. She was confused about morality because her parents said one thing and did the opposite. The therapist indicated that she could tell whether something was right or wrong for her by the way she felt afterwards. Miss C's promiscuity continued until she developed a steady relationship with a man who resembled her father in age and drinking habits. For a while this relationship gave Miss C enough security and stability to stop her one-night stands. But when the relationship began to sour, she resumed her old pattern, which her boyfriend tolerated.

When Miss C discussed her boyfriend's inconsiderate and degrading treatment of her, the therapist suggested the relationship could not continue that way forever. It would either have to improve or she would get strong enough to break it off. When Miss C discussed her distress over her sexual promiscuity, the therapist suggested that when she had a better relationship with either her present boyfriend or someone else, she would be able to give this up. All along the therapist kept expressing the belief that Miss C was worthy of a good relationship with a man and that she did not have to degrade herself or allow others to degrade her.

A few months after her individual treatment began, Miss C met a married professional man who wanted to take her out. She refused several invitations because it had been her policy not to date married men. However his persistence broke down her resolve and she finally accepted. Thus began the best relationship she had ever had with a man. He treated her decently and she was able to enjoy intercourse as she never had before. She felt sexually normal with him because he was "straight," not "perverted" like all the men she had known previously. Miss C was so satisfied with this man that she lost all interest in other men. She tried to break off with her old boyfriend, but he hung on to the relationship, insisting he would marry her in the end. He also started treating her much better than before, but this did not last. Miss C was torn between these two boyfriends for many months. At times she favored the married man because he treated her better and she enjoyed sex with him more. At other times she favored her old boyfriend because he had no other ties and she felt she could depend on him more. The married man said he wanted to marry her, but he could not bring himself to leave his family.

Eventually Miss C decided that her relationship with her old boyfriend was not good for her and she mustered all her strength to finally end it. For a while she also considered breaking off with her married boyfriend because she felt the relationship was a dead end for her. However she felt she was not strong enough to be completely alone, and so she decided to hold on to him until she found someone who could be committed to her. Accordingly, she started going out with other men, but in a manner totally different from her earlier pattern. Whereas she previously sought one-night stands, she now sought more lasting relationships and she was both selective and cautious before engaging in sexual relations. Jealous over her dating of others, her married boyfriend began to talk more and more about leaving his family for her. Since this made Miss C feel guilty as well as glad, she did not urge him to take this step. He eventually did leave his wife, but his relationship with Miss C didn't work out, so they stopped seeing each other altogether and he returned to his wife.

Even after their loose sexual behavior was brought under control, Mrs. B and Miss C still worried about their sexual fantasies, their past homosexual relations, and how these related to their adequacy in normal heterosexual relations.

The therapist sought to alleviate their anxieties about their fantasies by pointing out that they should not be ashamed of them since everyone has sexual fantasies. The important thing to realize is the difference between fantasy and reality, and just because they fantasize something does not mean it will actually happen in reality. Moreover, just because they have fantasized things they considered sexually abnormal does not mean they cannot also enjoy what they consider normal sex. This was proven to them when their sexual fantasies and anxieties subsided and they began to be satisfied in intercourse.

As for their fears about being lesbians, the therapist expressed the view that a few homosexual contacts do not necessarily mean that a person is a homosexual, and in their case, there was considerable evidence against their being true lesbians. For one thing, these experiences seem to have arisen more from their inability to say no than from their actively seeking such contact. For another, they were not currently seeking such contact. Both patients were greatly relieved on hearing these interpretations, and in a short while they stopped worrying about the possibility of being homosexual.

As Mrs. B and Miss C developed control over their acting out behavior and were reassured about their sexual normalcy, they focused increasingly on the more mundane details of their everyday lives. Mrs. B discussed her difficulties handling her son and getting along with her husband. She worried excessively over every little problem with her son because she had no idea what was normal and what was abnormal behavior in children, so limited was her contact with other mothers and their children. To help her with this problem, the therapist operated much as a friendly neighbor might in discussing children. In this way Mrs. B was relieved of many of her unnecessary worries. Those worries that seemed to the therapist to be real problems were discussed at length, and with the therapist's help she worked out better ways of coping with them. In similar ways Mrs. B worked to improve her relationship with her husband. It is interesting that at the end of treatment when the therapist asked Mrs. B to review what she had gained from therapy, she focused on these issues and forgot to mention gaining control of her acting out behavior. Evidently Mrs. B was so oriented to the present that the recent past seemed like ancient history to her.

Miss C had a lot of concerns about her relationship with her young daughter. She worried about the rejecting feelings she had toward her daughter in the past and the occasional return of these same feelings. She also worried about her loving feelings because she feared she was too dependent on her daughter. On the other hand, she felt little concern over one thing that would normally arouse considerable maternal concern, namely, her daughter's repeated exposure to violent scenes.

The therapist attempted to alleviate Miss C's guilt over her rejecting feelings by assuring her that it is natural for people to have ambivalent feelings toward their children and the fact that she sometimes felt rejecting toward her daughter did not mean that she did not also love her. As for her fears of being too dependent on her daughter, the therapist agreed that this was true since Miss C frequently reversed the parent-child roles (e.g., she would ask her daughter to enter a dark room first to make sure no one was in it). Accordingly, the therapist supported Miss C's efforts to act more like a parent. Finally the therapist tried to arouse more concern in Miss C about her daughter's exposure to violence in the hope that Miss C would exercise more control in these situations. The therapist's success in all these endeavors was very gradual, but eventually fairly complete.

Mrs. B's long-term treatment was terminated after 11 months because she felt strong enough to maintain the gains she had made in therapy, i.e., reduction of her anxiety, control of her drinking and sexual acting out behavior, elimination of her guilty depressions, an improved marital relationship, greater confidence in her mothering ability, and a greater sense of her own worth. It was understood that she could contact the therapist for further treatment if she ever felt the need for it. Several years have passed and Mrs. B still has not requested any further treatment.

Miss C's individual treatment continued for two and a half years during which she made further gains in achieving stability and security in her emotions, interpersonal relations, and employment. Toward the end of treatment, sessions were reduced in frequency and length until treatment was finally terminated when Miss C decided to move out of state to be closer to her family, who had just returned to the States after spending several years overseas. From occasional phone and letter communications, the therapist learned that Miss C continued to have many ups and downs in her life, but her overall functioning is far better than when she began treatment. She has been living with a man for several years and she has been employed for several months in a very good job.

Chapter 8

SCHIZOPHRENIA

CLINICAL DESCRIPTION

Schizophrenia is a psychotic thought disorder in which the individual turns away from the external world of reality toward an inner world of fantasy to such a degree that his perceptions and thoughts are dominated by inner wishes and fears and he cannot distinguish fantasy from reality. This break with reality is marked by some or all of the following symptoms: distorted perceptions, irrational ideas, bizarre fantasies, illogical reasoning, and peculiar language. In addition to this split with reality, there is a split between affect and thought. The schizophrenic's affect is usually flat so that he can discuss normally upsetting issues without any visible sign of emotion. But at times the schizophrenic is overly excitable and can become violent over minor upsets. In this as everything, the schizophrenic goes from one extreme to another. Schizophrenics see everything in absolute black and white terms, without any shades of gray. At times they are overly abstract and their associations are so loose that they link widely disparate objects and events because of minute resemblances. At other times, they are overly concrete and their interpretations are so literal that they completely miss real meanings. In many cases the behavior of a schizophrenic is so extreme that even untrained observers realize something is amiss.

While schizophrenia is widely viewed as a unitary dysfunction because of its general features, it has been categorized into different types according to specific symptoms (simple, paranoid, catatonic, hebephrenic, undifferentiated), premorbid adjustment (good vs. poor), speed of onset (insidious vs. acute), and length of illness (acute vs. chronic).

These are observations about schizophrenia which most people in the mental health field would agree upon. However, the question of the nature and origin of schizophrenia is another matter. In this there is no general agreement.

INTERPRETATIONS OF SCHIZOPHRENIA*

Medical Model.   According to the medical model, schizophrenia is a mental illness caused by some as yet undetermined organic factor and treatable by medication.

Psychoanalytic Model.   According to the psychoanalytic model, schizophrenia is a severe emotional disturbance stemming from early problems in psychosexual development. Treatment is primarily through psychotherapy aimed at providing a corrective emotional experience.

Family Interaction Model.   According to the family interaction model (Bateson, Haley, Wynne, Singer, Lidz), the schizophrenic is the family member who has been chosen by the family to act out the family's pathology. Treatment is conducted with the whole family to break down the family pathology and thereby to free the patient from his "crazy" role.

* This section is largely derived from: Siegler, and Osmond, *Models of Madness*, Br. J. Psychiatry, 1966, 112:1193-1203.

Moral Model.   According to the moral model (Glasser), schizophrenia is nothing more than socially unacceptable behavior. Labeling it an illness is unwise because it gives the individual an excuse to continue his irresponsible behavior. Treatment is aimed at increasing the patient's socially acceptable behavior by controlling his environment, by setting up a system of rewards for acceptable behavior, and by urging him to behave more responsibly.

Phenomenological Model.   According to the phenomenological model (Laing, Esterson), there is no such thing as a "schizophrenic condition." So-called schizophrenics are persons with peculiar experiences and behavior which are fully intelligible in light of family events (particularly, disconfirmations and mystifications of the patient). Treatment is aimed at altering the family events associated with the patient's peculiar experiences and behavior.

Although these models sound mutually exclusive, in practice they are often used in conjunction with each other. For example, many state hospitals combine the medical model with the moral model in a treatment program of medication and strict control of the environment, with increased freedom for "good" behavior. The medical model can also be combined with the psychoanalytic model to provide a treatment plan of medication and psychotherapy to deal with the physical and emotional aspects of the disorder. The psychoanalytic model is sometimes combined with the family interaction model in a treatment plan of individual and family therapy. The phenomenological model is a variant of the family interaction model and their treatment approaches are very similar.

SEARCHING FOR THE ETIOLOGY OF SCHIZOPHRENIA

At this time there are many data from many fields of research for each of these theories, but no conclusive evidence for any of them. The problem with schizophrenia research is the difficulty in determining whether a variable shown to be significantly related to schizophrenia is a cause, a result, or simply a concomitant factor. Longitudinal study of every aspect of development on a randomly selected population of thousands is necessary to determine which variables are most related to schizophrenia and whether they arose before, during, or after the onset of the disorder.

The number of significant findings in different fields suggests that schizophrenia is multidetermined, whether or not it is basically a single entity. It has not yet been shown whether schizophrenia is a unitary disorder arrived at by different pathways or a group of similar disorders with different causes. It is also possible that there is one variable that is a necessary, but not sufficient, factor in causing schizophrenia, while a whole range of variables serve as accompanying causes.

Even though the nature and etiology of schizophrenia has not yet been determined, it is still possible to successfully treat this disorder (or group of disorders). Each of the theories has some value in understanding and treating schizophrenia. The object is to find the model that best suits you, the therapist, and the patients you work with.

TREATING SCHIZOPHRENIA

Medication

In the author's experience, medication is often needed before psychotherapy can begin. While there are some rare therapists (like John Rosen) who can work through the psychosis by participating in it, most therapists prefer to work with the patient on the familiar grounds of reality. Using medication does not necessarily imply an acceptance of the organic theory of schizophrenia. For it is certainly possible that the physiological changes that the medication treats are caused by emotional disturbances.

Individual Relationship Therapy

As for the type of psychotherapy to be employed, the author has found individual relationship therapy to be most effective. In this treatment the patient is provided with a figure in reality to whom he can relate and whom he can learn to trust. To build this relationship the therapist behaves in a warm, friendly, supportive manner. The therapist discourages prolonged discussions of the patient's fantasies by refusing to get involved in them and by focussing instead on practical everyday issues in reality.

The past is similarly avoided in favor of the present as a topic for discussion. When confrontations are necessary, they are made in as nonthreatening a manner as possible, with the therapist's basic acceptance of the patient made perfectly clear. Trying to convince the patient of the irrationality of his thinking works only in the initial stages of schizophrenia. After that it should be avoided because it is wasted effort. Through the relationship and discussions, the patient regains interest in external reality and begins relating to other people as well as to the therapist.

In a sense, the therapist serves as a bridge to the outside world.

Group Therapy

Group therapy can be used as an adjunct to individual therapy to increase the schizophrenic's socialization. It is particularly effective for groups of chronic schizophrenics to have group therapy with a recreational focus. On the other hand, group therapy as the sole means of treatment is not very effective with schizophrenics, particularly in mixed groups of patients. While the benefits of socialization afforded by group therapy are most desperately needed by schizophrenics, unfortunately they are the patients least able to partake of these benefits.

Family Therapy

A similar problem exists with family therapy. The severe pathology seen in many families of schizophrenics indicates the desparate need for changes in family interaction. Unfortunately this severe pathology often works against successful family treatment. Ironically, families with less severe pathology usually benefit more from family therapy than the schizophrenic's family, in whom the need for change is greatest. This does not mean that family therapy should not be attempted with families of schizophrenics. It simply means that before attempting such treatment, the therapist should recognize that individual therapy aimed at helping the schizophrenic gain independence from his family's pathology might be a quicker and more effective form of treatment than family therapy. The age of the patient should be considered before a decision is made for or against family therapy. In general it is more useful for younger patients who are not yet old enough to leave home.

Behavior Modification

Behavior modification can be very useful in improving the level of functioning of hospitalized chronic schizophrenics, as well as in suppressing the more flamboyant symptoms in acute schizophrenia. As such, its effect is very much like that of medication. It can suppress symptoms and improve functioning, but in the author's opinion, it is far from a cure.

Reasoning

Reasoning with a schizophrenic to get him to behave more acceptably can work at times, but in the author's opinion this happens best in the context of a warm relationship, and as such, can be considered as one more method in relationship therapy.

The following case of schizophrenia was treated by individual relationship therapy and medication.

CASE REPORT OF A SCHIZOPHRENIC PATIENT

The patient, Mrs. R, was a 40-year-old mother of two teenage girls who had been seen in couples therapy with her husband a year and a half before the onset of this schizophrenic episode.

The couples therapy dealt with a severe rift in their relationship which had been present to some degree from the early years of their marriage, but which had grown larger when the wife became ill with a thyroid condition. For several months she largely ceased functioning in her housewife role and household chores were done haphazardly by her husband and daughters. In addition, Mrs. R's moods were very erratic. Couples therapy began at a point close to divorce; the husband was saying he couldn't take his wife's behavior anymore and the wife was saying she couldn't stand his lack of affection and lack of support. However the fact that neither really wanted a divorce was evidenced by their rapid agreement to a therapy contract to work on keeping their marriage. The wife further demonstrated her desire to save the marriage by her recent recovery from her illness and her religious faith that she was through being sick. Although the wife displayed certain bizarre elements in her thinking, there was no clear evidence of psychosis at this time. The couple mentioned some sort of breakdown after the birth of their first child 14 years before, but it was not clear whether she had been actually psychotic. At the time of the couples treatment, the therapist saw Mrs. R as someone with a very fragile ego and a real psychotic potential, but without an actual psychosis.

Since the husband and wife both wanted to maintain the marriage, the couples therapy proceeded quite well. In a few months the focus of treatment shifted from restoration of the marriage to its improvement. One thing Mr. and Mrs. R had to chuckle about was how they each tried to think for one another and do for each other what they felt the other needed, regardless of what the other really wanted. In the course of therapy they learned how to send and receive messages more clearly as well as how to work together to solve some of their common problems with children and parents. After eight months of treatment, therapy ended on a positive note with the couple feeling that while they were not over all their problems, they were now working together and could manage without therapy.

A year and a half later, Mrs. R contacted the therapist for an appointment for her eldest daughter. After two sessions with the daughter which were interrupted by Mrs. R expressing concerns not only about her daughter, but about her marriage as well, it was very obvious that while her daughter was in a highly nervous state, Mrs. R needed therapy even more and was most likely the cause of her daughter's nervousness. Mrs. R denied any need for treatment for herself, but agreed to alternate sessions with her daughter so she could discuss her "daughter's" problems. At this point Mrs. R arranged for her sister also to see the therapist and to discuss the sister's problems. While the sister did have some problems, she was not particularly interested in treatment and had kept the appointment only to humor Mrs. R. Accordingly, the therapist told Mrs. R that her sister's problems were not as pressing as Mrs. R had believed. In fact her own problems were more pressing and she needed therapy more than her sister, whereupon Mrs. R finally agreed to weekly appointments for herself and to have her daughter seen only occasionally by the therapist.

At the next session Mrs. R was extremely confused and incoherent. Accordingly, she was referred to a psychiatrist for medication, so communication could be facilitated. While this medication slowed her thinking down somewhat, it did not eliminate her psychotic thoughts. (She still showed confusion, loss of memory, and paranoid ideation.) Over the next few months the patient had many emotional upheavals related to her psychotic thinking.

For example, she left home to take care of a sick woman who was remotely related to her and insisted on staying with this woman despite her husband's urging that she come home to take care of her own family, and despite this remote relative's telling her she was no longer needed. She was finally forced to leave when the woman called the police to remove her from her home. Mrs. R was very hurt by this brutal rejection of her kindness, but she salvaged her pride by explaining it away as an indication of how mentally ill this relative was. The therapist sympathized with Mrs. R's hurt feelings and agreed that the relative's action was extremè. However, the therapist also pointed out how stubborn Mrs. R had been not to leave when she was told she was no longer needed and that she brought this situation on herself by ignoring her relative's wishes. Mrs. R could see this and she agreed with the therapist's suggestion that in the future she should be less insistent on forcing her kind intentions on other people. The therapist also went on to interpret her desire to be helpful to her relative in terms of her own need to be needed, which was less and less satisfied as her children grew older. Mrs. R agreed with this and brought up other needs of hers which were not being satisfied by her husband, primarily her need for affection.

Mrs. R then went on and on about the basic incompatibility of her husband and herself, which she attributed to their astrological signs. In a short time she stopped talking about her husband's actual behavior and relied solely on astrology to prove what a terrible person he was. Mrs. R also started bringing books on astrology for the therapist to read. The therapist handled this by agreeing to read the books, but making it clear where she stood on the issue of astrology. As the therapist saw it, there is a whole array of attitudes about astrology ranging from complete acceptance to complete rejection, with partial acceptance and interest but reserved judgment somewhere in between. Mrs. R had recently moved from partial to complete acceptance, while the theraptist remained in the category of being interested in it, but not really believing it. Mrs. R accepted this difference and did not get upset whenever the therapist tried to bring the discussion away from astrology toward actual events. When Mrs. R couldn't really find many things to support her belief that her husband was a terrible person, she changed her opinion and started saying he was basically a good person, it was just that he was not her type. The therapist indicated that while they may clash in many areas, they were getting along fairly well a year and half ago at the end of the couples therapy, and she should consider having her husband join her in therapy. Mrs. R did not like this idea at all. She started saying she was allergic to her husband. He was making her sick and she needed to be free of him to get well. Soon after that, Mrs. R told her husband to leave home, at least until she got better.

With her husband out of the home, Mrs. R began focusing all her attention on her oldest daughter. She started intruding into her daughter's social life and became inappropriately in- volved in trying to promote her daughter's relationship with a boy whom the girl had a crush on, including phoning the boy's parents to discuss the situation and at one point blurt- ing out that her daughter was emotionally disturbed and in the care of a psychologist. The daughter was naturally humiliated by her mother's behavior, but she didn't know how to handle it, particularly since all her friends liked her mother and found her astrology interests fascinating. When the therapist tried to have Mrs. R see how she had upset her daughter, Mrs. R could recognize it intellectually, but it did not really sink in emotionally. Finally this daughter started staying over at friends' houses more than at home. At the same time Mrs. R's housekeeping markedly deteriorated so that the home had become chaotic.

Mr. R offered to come home to help Mrs. R out or to take over while Mrs. R went to a hospital or to her mother's. At first Mrs. R adamantly refused all thse alternatives, but after discussing them with the therapist she realized she had to leave the home for her children's sake, and she agreed to move out temporarily and stay with her mother until she pulled herself together.

A month or so later, relieved of all her responsibilities, Mrs. R had calmed down considerably and was no longer displaying flamboyant psychotic behavior, though she was still very tense and emotional. Accordingly, she attempted to negotiate her return to the home and her husband's departure. Her husband said she could return, but he refused to leave. Thus began a painful battle with her husband that lasted for the next year and a half. Mrs. R adamantly refused to live under the same roof with her husband, because she felt his lack of affection was largely responsible for her breakdown. However, she did not want to give up her children and she sought legal help to regain custody of them. Her lawyer delayed court action for a year and a half until she was more emotionally stable and had a better chance of regaining custody.

This was a very difficult year and a half for Mrs. R, but she worked very hard to pull herself together. She found her visits with her children very painful because of the inevitable parting, but she also recognized that she wasn't really ready to take on the full responsibility of their care. She had many ups and downs with her favorite older daughter, but her relationship with her husband's favorite, the younger daughter, steadily improved. This was a source of great satisfaction and comfort to her. Mrs. R's relationship with her mother also steadily improved from the stormy days of her breakdown.

By the time the divorce and custody case came to court, Mrs. R felt she had little chance of winning the custody battle because of her psychiatric history and because she had not become stable enought to secure and hold a job. However, by this time Mrs. R wasn't so sure that it was such a good idea for her to have custody of the children. They seemed to be doing fine and she had settled into a pleasant routine of visiting them and enjoying their company without the responsibility of their care. Therefore, she took it quite well when the court ruled in favor of her husband keeping the children with him.

Soon after that, Mrs. R found a job as an assistant to a man who had a small free-lance business. A romance developed between them and they decided to get married. At her last therapy session, Mrs. R reviewed the events of the past two years and how far she had come. She had been completely off medication for over two months and was feeling better than ever. She was very happy with her fiance because he had all the warmth that she found lacking in her husband. With his help she felt sure that she could manage to take care of her children, but she wasn't so sure that she wanted to take on the responsibility now that she was enjoying her freedom to come and go with her fiance. However she was increasing her visits with her children and was very pleased to see how much they liked her fiance and how much he liked them. As for her interest in astrology, it had subsided greatly. She was too busy with her fiance's business to have much time for astrology.

Chapter 9

SUICIDE RISKS

Even though many people have thoughts of suicide without ever attempting to kill themselves, and even though many suicide gestures are pleas for attention rather than sincere attempts, the therapist must never treat the mention of suicide lightly. The fact remains that most successful suicides are preceded by warnings that were not sufficiently heeded, and histories of repeated unsuccessful suicide attempts often end in actual suicide. Moreover, it is undeniable that any suicidal gesture for attention may accidentally result in death. The therapist should also be aware that no one is ever completely suicidal. No matter how intense the wish to die, there is a coexisting wish to live. Otherwise, why do people give warnings and seek help before they commit suicide? Furthermore, no matter how intense the wish to die, the feeling is not constant. Otherwise, why are so many seriously suicidal people grateful after they have been saved?

The first thing a therapist should do when a patient expresses thoughts of suicide is to evaluate the immediacy of the suicidal danger.

- What are the patient's reasons for wanting to commit suicide?
- How strong is the patient's wish for death?
- Does the patient have the means at her disposal?
- Does the patient have a history of previous suicidal attempts?

If there is an immediate danger of suicide, the patient should be hospitalized for her own protection. Because of the unpredictablity of their behavior, psychotic suicidal patients should also be hospitalized, whether or not there is an immediate danger of suicide.

Even if the patient doesn't like the ideal of hospitalization, she will usually recognize the need for inpatient treatment and agree to enter a hospital voluntarily. Only rarely is it necessary to arrange for a period of involuntary hospitalization. Different states have different laws governing involuntary hospitalizations and every therapist should be aware of the legal procedures in her state.

If a therapist is uncertain about the immediacy of the suicidal danger or the presence of psychosis, she should not hesitate to consult with a colleague.

If the danger of suicide is not immediate and the patient is rational, the therapist can conduct treatment on an outpatient basis, with psychiatric consultation to determine the advisability of antidepressant medication. In addition, to insure the safety of the patient, the therapist and patient can make the following kind of contract:

1. The therapist agrees to work with the patient on an outpatient basis to overcome the patient's suicidal feelings. The frequency of the sessions will depend upon the intensity of the patient's wish to die.
2. The patient agrees to give therapy a fair chance and not to make any suicidal attempts for the duration of

therapy. (It is very effective to point out to the patient that by trying therapy she is not giving up her chance to commit suicide later on. But if she commits suicide now, she will give up forever her chance in therapy to make a happier life for herself.)

3. If at any time during treatment the patient feels strongly suicidal, she will contact the therapist to discuss her feelings and decide whether hospitalization is advisable.

4. If the therapist is not immediately available and the patient feels she cannot wait to talk to the therapist, the patient will go to the emergency room of a local hospital to consult with the doctor on call, who will handle the problem by discussion and/or medication and/or hospitalization.

5. If the patient's demands for the therapist's time are more than the therapist can handle on an outpatient basis, the patient will have to be hospitalized so she can be treated as an inpatient.

Once these conditions are agreed upon, therapy can begin with a thorough exploration of (1) the patient's reasons for wanting to kill herself; (2) the things the patient has done thus far to alleviate her problems, and (3) how successful she has been. Then the therapist can point out other alternatives open to the patient and support the patient as she tries some of these alternatives and begins to renew her interest in life.

Chapter 10

MARITAL THERAPY

As in other forms of psychotherapy, the establishment of a therapeutic relationship is essential before any treatment can begin. In marital therapy the situation is complicated by the fact that both marital partners often come to treatment with the goal of winning an ally to their side of the conflict. The therapist must demonstrate a fair-minded commitment to work on improving the relationship for the benefit of both partners. When the therapist shows understanding for one partner's predicament, he should also show understanding of the other partner's point of view. When the therapist seems to side with one partner, he should point out how a change will also benefit the other partner in the long run. When the therapist points out a problem that one partner needs to work on, he should point out a similar or opposite problem that the other partner needs to work on. In these ways the therapist demonstrates that he is the ally of both. At the same time the therapist is helping each partner increase his or her understanding of the other partner's feelings.

If the degree of hostility between a couple seems overwhelming at times, the therapist should remember that on some level, the marital partners must care about each other. Otherwise, how would they have managed to stay together so long in the face of their intense conflicts and why would they come for marital therapy? The therapist should not only remember this himself, but at strategic moments he should also remind the couple of this.

No two marital conflicts are exactly alike. Nevertheless, there are certain patterns that run through many different conflicts. The following section describes five patterns (which may appear independently or together) and suitable methods of therapeutic intervention for each.

PATTERNS OF CONFLICTS

Vicious Cycle of Escalating Hostilities

A does something that annoys B. B retaliates with words or behavior designed to hurt or anger A, who in turn retaliates with similarly hostile words or behavior. So it goes on and on, until a vicious cycle of escalating hostilities is firmly established. Oftentimes a couple does not even know when and how it all began.

Couples caught in such a cycle of excessively expressed hostility need to learn to control their anger and to become more careful in communicating their grievances. The therapist can help such a couple reverse this vicious cycle by pointing out what is going on and by encouraging the couple to discuss their basic differences calmly. Eventually the couple should be able to maintain themselves at a lower, more manageable level of anger. If this cannot be accomplished through discussion, the therapist can help break the impasse by setting new rules for the expression of feelings. For example, the therapist might prescribe that all fighting must cease outside the therapy hour. Grievances should be written down and saved for the next session. In addition, the therapist might prescribe that each partner say one nice thing about the other in the session or do one nice thing for the other during the week. Of course, the couple must be thoroughly committed to treatment to be willing to cooperate in this. It is striking how many extremely hostile couples are willing to carry out these behavioral prescriptions and even more impressive how effective these methods are. For one thing, it gives the couple a breathing space where they can begin to enjoy each other's company again. For another, it brings to the surface long-hidden positive feelings for each other. In all likelihood, the success of these methods rests in large part on the couple's feeling that this may be their only chance to restore their severely damaged relationship.

Conflicts Over Diametrically Opposed Attitudes

Many couples have diametrically opposed ways of doing things and they look to a therapist to judge which is the best way, with each partner believing that his or her way will win. These couples are quite surprised when the therapist refuses to take sides as they imagined he would, and instead points out the good and bad in each extreme while suggesting that a compromise between extremes would probably be the best way of all. Couples usually respond to this approach very well because even though no one has won, neither have they lost. Then with the help of the therapist they can work on figuring out compromises satisfactory to both. While this may require a lot of work, it often is not difficult at all. In these cases a compromise solution was really quite at hand, if only the couple had bothered to look for it.

Supersensitivity to a Trait in One's Spouse While Being Unaware of the Same Trait in Oneself

Whereas the previous situation reflects the popular principle that opposites attract, this situation is related to the psycho-analytic principle that people seek relationships at their own level. A good way of handling this problem is to point out the striking similarities and parallels in the couple's behavior. Although there may be some resistance to recognizing this, couples usually respond to this approach with shared surprise and amusement. Furthermore, since they have already experienced what it is like to be on the receiving end of their kind of behavior, they are usually very willing to work on changing it. Treatment can then proceed in a straightforward manner, with the couple exploring alternative ways of be-having, appreciating improvements, and guarding against reversions to former behavior.

Suppressed Anger Leading to Passive-Aggressive Behavior

In this situation A is afraid to express openly his anger toward B and therefore keeps things in. While some annoy-ances pass, others build up until they are expressed in in-direct, hurtful ways. This is very unfair to B and to the whole relationship because B has no idea what B is doing to aggra-vate A and is therefore unable to remedy the situation. Of course, B may be similarly suppressing anger and expressing it in indirect ways. This is a case of too little communication of real feelings.

This difficulty can be handled therapeutically by pointing out what is going on below the surface and by encouraging the couple to bring their feelings to the surface. Then with the help of the therapist they can learn to deal with them more effectively.

Partner Means Well But Unwittingly Hurts the Other

This situation results from incomplete communication in the transmission or reception of messages. A tries to please B, but never really knows what B wants. This may happen because B is too reserved in expressing wishes, and/or because A sees B's needs in terms of his own needs and therefore doesn't even try to find out what B wants.

The therapist should point out the couple's incomplete communication and encourage the couple to fill in the gaps by communicating more openly and asking more questions.

POSSIBLE DIVORCE

In concluding this chapter on marital therapy, something must be said about the possibility of divorce. When a couple comes for treatment to save their marriage, the therapist naturally does everything he can to help the couple achieve this goal. However, in the course of treatment, it may become clearer and clearer to the therapist that there is not a true committment to saving the marriage on the part of one or both partners. If this happens the therapist should point out the evidence and help the partners face up to and adjust to reality. Individual sessions with either or both partners might be called for.

Whatever the outcome of marital therapy, the therapist should remember that his role is to help the couple define their goals and work toward them, regardless of what they turn out to be. The therapist should not be so invested in saving the marriage that he feels like a failure if the couple decides that is not what they really want.

Chapter 11

SEXUAL DYSFUNCTIONS

Treatment of sexual dysfunctions requires, first of all, a thorough evaluation of the nature of the problem, including sexual history, time of onset of the problem, and its effect on sexual activity. In the course of this evaluation, the various intrapsychic and interpersonal factors involved in the dysfunction will come to light.

EVALUATION OF THE PROBLEM

Time of Onset

One obvious dimension is the time of the onset of the problem, whether (1) it was present from the start of the sexual relationship, or (2) it arose immediately after the wedding despite satisfactory premarital relations, or (3) it developed after years of marriage.

108

rience, or faulty learning on the part of one or both partners. These in turn can be traced to negative or distorted ideas about sex that were developed during childhood and adolescence. No matter how sound the original relationship, the long continuance of sexual dysfunction tends to blight other areas of the relationship. Examples of these early-appearing problems are erective difficulties and premature ejaculation in the male, and dyspareunia (painful intercourse), vaginismus, and lack of orgasm in the female. Gradual relearning about sex in a relaxed atmosphere is necessary to overcome these primary dysfunctions.

When there is a marked decline in sexual desire immediately following the wedding even though the couple had a history of satisfactory premarital relations, there appears to be a deep intrapsychic conflict over autonomy and freedom vs. control and obligation. In other words, the individual who enjoyed sex in the unmarried state when it was given freely, without obligation, suddenly loses interest in sex when it becomes a requirement of marriage. The solution to this problem lies in helping the patient become aware of and resolve this conflict, as well as in gradually reawakening the individual's sexual interest in the spouse.

Sexual problems that develop after years of marriage are usually the result of interpersonal difficulties in the marriage and a breakdown of marital communication. Infrequent sexual desire is a prime example of this kind of problem, but erective and orgasmic difficulties can also appear. Improvement in the marital communications and a working through of interpersonal conflict is needed, as well as unpressured reintroduction to sexual pleasure.

Starting—Finishing

Another dimension along which these same dysfunctions can be divided is the starting-finishing dimension.

Some persons have difficulty getting started in a sexual encounter because they have infrequent desire for sex and are not easily aroused; however, once aroused they have no trouble in engaging in a completely satisfying relationship. This situation is very hard for the spouse to understand, and the spouse usually ends up feeling a combination of anger over the frustration and hurt over the rejection. Moreover, the longer the problem continues, the stronger the spouse's felt need for sex, which in turn increases the tension between the couple. Once the situation is improved, the spouse may discover his or her need for sex was not as great as previously believed.

The solution to this problem lies in discovering the sources of resistance to arousal and working them through. This varies with each case. For example, in one case a husband sought sex only after he was physiologically aroused. He never wanted his wife to stimulate him to arousal. He seemed to fear failure if he was not in total command of the situation from the start. He needed to learn that it was perfectly all right for him to be aroused by his wife and to discover that he could function in that situation. In another case the wife's sexual responsiveness followed a rigid pattern. If anything upset that pattern she would lose all interest. She superstitiously feared failure if things did not develop according to her. accustomed mode of operation. She needed to try greater flexibility in her lovemaking and to discover that she could respond adequately even when she did not follow her accustomed pattern.

In the opposite situation, the individual has no trouble becoming aroused, but has difficulty successfully completing the sex act, i.e., the male is so easily excited he nearly always ejaculates prematurely; the female is easily aroused to orgasm through manipulation but can't relax enough to permit entry or she can be aroused to seek intercourse but not to the point of orgasm. Depending upon the duration of the problem and the spouse's patience and self-confidence, the spouse reacts to the problem with either sympathy, self-blame, or anger. The dysfunctional individuals suffer from intense feelings of inadequacy and desparately try to overcome the problem. Unfortunately, through their eagerness and lack of knowledge, they often finish by doing things that not only do not help the situation, but actually make matters worse. For example, in trying to delay ejaculation one man would imagine the approaching ejaculation so vividly he would bring it on all the more quickly. The more common reaction of trying to think of other things also does not work because a man can't control ejaculation when he is distracted. The premature ejaculator must be made aware of the approaching ejaculation so that he can control it, but he must also be taught to relax and go slowly. The squeeze technique simultaneously accomplishes both of these goals. Another example is a case of vaginismus in which the couple was so eager to have intercourse they repeatedly attempted entry after very brief foreplay. It was necessary for them to slow down their lovemaking and to attempt insertion gradually. Still another example is the common one of the nonorgasmic woman concentrating so hard on achieveing her goal that she doesn't experience the mounting excitement which would naturally and effortlessly bring about orgasm. These women must learn to focus on the immediate sensual experience instead of an end goal. In some cases they must learn to do this by themselves before they can do it with a partner.

METHODS OF TREATMENT

Once the evaluation is completed, an appropriate treatment plan can be devised using any or all of the following methods.

Sexual Education to Correct Misinformation

This is a straightforward method utilizing verbal explanations and/or assignment of reading materials.

Sensual and Sexual Exercises to Enhance Sexual Responsivity

Certain exercises apply to all types of dysfunctions. The well-known sensate focus exercise devised by Masters and Johnson is a useful technique for all types of dysfunctions. This exercise reduces anxiety in patients whose sexual functioning is hindered by anxiety about sexual performance. At the same time it permits the natural awakening (or reawakening) of sexual desires in persons who are sexually inhibited for one reason or another. Use of erotic fantasy is another technique applicable to all kinds of dysfunctions. The individual is instructed to fantasize sexually stimulating situations prior to and during sexual activities. If the individual cannot develop his own fantasies, he is instructed to read erotic literature. Fantasy works not only to increase arousal, but also diverts attention from performance anxieties.

Examples of specific techniques for specific problems are the squeeze technique for premature ejaculation, gradual dilation for vaginismus, and manual stimulation for lack of orgasm. It is not in the province of this book to describe these techniques in detail. However, the reader can refer to Belliveau and Richter's *Understanding Human Sexual Inadequacy* (New York: Bantam Books, 1970) for an excellent summary of the Masters and Johnson techniques.

Working Through Intrapsychic Conflicts

Most intrapsychic conflicts about sex can be overcome in the course of re-education about sex and participation in sexual exercises. However some conflicts are so deeply entrenched that individual therapy is necessary before they can be overcome.

Working Through Interpersonal Conflicts

Sex therapy with couples deals with their total communication, not just their sexual relationship. Accordingly, it involves ordinary couple counseling to improve communication and ways of handling conflicts. In some cases the interpersonal conflicts are so severe that it is necessary to do extensive couple therapy before embarking on a program of sexual therapy.

DEALING WITH DYSFUNCTIONS THAT ARE RESISTANT TO TREATMENT

In conclusion, one additional point should be made. When a particular sexual dysfunction is very resistant to treatment, the therapist should keep in mind that sexual functioning is a natural phenomenon, not an extraordinary achievement. Therefore, if one treatment method doesn't work, some other method is bound to succeed. The therapist's hopeful attitude and commitment to work on the problem until it is solved is of inestimable value in helping the patient relax and gain enough confidence to allow treatment to succeed eventually.

BIBLIOGRAPHY.

Akerman, N., Beatmen, F., and Sherman, S., *Expanding Theory and Practice in Family Therapy*, New York: Family Service Association of America, 1967.

Arieti, S., *Interpretations of Schizophrenia*, New York: Brunner, 1955.

Arieti, S. (Ed.), *American Handbook of Psychiatry*, New York: Basic Books, 1959.

Bach, G., and Wyden, P., *The Intimate Enemy*, New York: Avon Books, 1968.

Bateson, G., Jackson, D., Haley, J., and Weakland, J., *Toward a Theory of Schizophrenia*, Behavioral Science, 1956, 1:251-264.

Belliveau, F., and Richter, L., *Understanding Human Sexual Inadequacy*, New York: Bantam Book, 1970.

Berne, E., *Games People Play*, New York: Grove Press, 1964.

*Bettelheim, B., *Love is Not Enough*, New York: Free Press, 1950.

Bibring, E., Psychoanalysis and the dynamic psychotherapies, Journal of the American Psychoanalytic Association, 1954, 2:745-77.

*Brenner, C., *An Elementary Textbook of Psychoanalysis*, New York: International Universities Press, 1955.

*Cleckley, H., *The Mask of Sanity*, Saint Louis: C.V. Mosby Co., 1964.

*Highly recommended.

*Deutsch, F., and Murphy, W., *The Clinical Interview*, New York: International Universities Press.

Ellis, A., *Reason and Emotion in Psychotherapy*, New York: Lyle Stuart, 1962.

*Erikson, E., *Childhood and Society*, New York: Norton, 1950.

Erikson, E., *Identity and the Life Cycle*, Psychological Issues, 1959, 1, Monogr. No. 1.

Fagan, J., and Shepherd, I., *Gestalt Therapy Now*, New York: Harper Colophon Books, 1970.

Fenichel, O., *The Psychoanalytic Theory of Neurosis*, New York: Norton, 1945.

Frailberg, S., *The Magic Years*, New York: Charles Scribner's Sons, 1959.

*Freud, A., *The Ego and the Mechanisms of Defense*, New York: International Universities Press, 1946.

Freud, S., *Collected Papers, Vol. 1-5*, London: Hogarth Press, 1925.

Freud, S., *The Interpretations of Dreams*, Basic Writings, New York: The Modern Library, 1938.

*Fromm-Reichman, F., *Principles of Intensive Psychotherapy*, Chicago: University of Chicago Press, 1950.

Gill, M., Psychoanalysis and exploratory psychotherapy, Journal of the American Association, 1954, 2:771-797.

Glasser, W., *Reality Therapy*, New York: Harper & Row, 1965.

Glover, E., Psychoanalysis and psychotherapy, British Journal of Medical Psychology, 1960, 33:73-82.

Green, R., *Sexual Identity and Conflict in Children and Adults*, New York: Basic Books, Inc., 1974.

Hall, C., and Lindzey, G., *Theories of Personality*, New York: John Wiley and Sons, 1957.

Jackson, D., *The Etiology of Schizophrenia*, New York: Basic Books, 1960.

*Jourard, S., *The Transparent Self*, Princeton: Van Nostrand, 1964.

Kaplan, H., *The New Sex Therapy*, New York: Brunner/Mazel Publishers, 1974.

Kubler-Ross, E., *On Death and Dying*, New York: Macmillan Publishing Co., 1970.

*Laing, R., and Esterson, A., *Sanity, Madness and the Family*, New York: Basic Books, 1964.

Laughlin, H., *The Ego and Its Defenses*, New York: Appleton-Century-Crofts, 1970.

Lidz, T., Fleck, S., and Cornelison, A., *Schizophrenia and the Family*, New York: International Universities Press, 1965.

Limentani, D., *Symbiotic Identification in Schizophrenia*, Psychiatry, 1956, 12:231-236.

*Loew, C., Grayson, H., and Loew, G., *Three Psychotherapies*, New York: Brunner/Mazel Publishers, 1975.

Mahler, M., Autism and symbiosis: Two extreme disturbances of identity, International Journal of Psychoanalysis, 1958, 39:77-83.

Marmor, J., Dynamic psychotherapy and behavior therapy, Archives of General Psychiatry, 1971, 24:22-28.

Masters, W., and Johnson, V., *Human Sexual Response*, Boston: Little, Brown & Co., 1965.

Mikulas, W., *Behavior Modification: An Overview*, New York: Harper & Row, 1972.

Morris, G., and Wynne, L., *Schizophrenic Offspring and Parental Styles of Communication*, Psychiatry, 1965, 28:17-44.

*Murphy, W., *The Tactics of Psychotherapy*, New York: International Universities Press, 1965.

Redl, F., and Wineman, D., *Children Who Hate*, New York: Free Press, 1951.

*Reich, W., *Character Analysis*, New York: Noonday Press, 1949.

*Reik, T., *Listening with the Third Ear*, New York: Farrar, Straus, 1948.

Rosen, J., *Direct Analysis*, New York: Grune & Stratton, 1953.

Ryckoff, I., Day, J., and Wynne, L., Maintenance of stereotyped roles in the families of schizophrenics, Archives of General Psychiatry, 1959, 1:93-98.

*Satir, V., *Conjoint Family Therapy*, Palo Alto: Palo Alto Science and Behavior Books, Inc., 1967.

Schneidman, E., Farberow, N., and Litman, R., *The Psychology of Suicide*, New York: Science House, 1970.

Siegler, M., and Osmond, H., Models of madness, British Journal of Psychiatry, 1966, 112:1193-1203.

Steiner, C., *Scripts People Live*, New York: Grove Press, 1974.

Wynne, L., Ryckoff, I., Day, J., and Hirsch, S., Pseudo-mutuality in the family relations of schizophrenics, Psychiatry, 1958, 21:205-220.

Zilboorg, G., Ambulatory schizophrenia, Psychiatry, 1941, 4:149-155.